BIZ JETS

BUSINESS & CORPORATE AIRCRAFT

Peter R. March

IAN ALLAN
Publishing

CONTENTS

First published 1996

ISBN 0 7110 2426 X

Published by Ian Allan Publishing
an imprint of Ian Allan Ltd,
Terminal House, Station Approach,
Shepperton, Surrey TW17 8AS.

Printed by Ian Allan Printing Ltd,
Coombelands House, Coombelands Lane,
Addlestone, Surrey KT15 1HY.

Front cover: Dassault Falcon 900B. **Dassault Aviation**

Back cover: Cessna 650 Citation III. **PRM**

Title page: Dassault Falcon 20B. **DJM**

Above: Raytheon/Hawker 1000. **via PRM**

Introduction

This first edition of *abc Biz Jets: Business & Corporate Aircraft* has been produced in series with *abc Civil Airliner Recognition, abc Light Aircraft Recognition* and *abc Classic & Warbird Recognition*. The four titles together comprehensively cover the majority of civil aircraft likely to be seen flying in Europe and North America.

Aircraft described in this recognition guide are mainly less than 30 years old, examples of which are owned and operated by private companies for their own benefit. The small and medium-size 'Biz Jet' — business or executive jet — and the larger corporate jets are included, together with the growing number of turboprops used in an executive/corporate capacity around the world. Also included are numerous piston-engined aircraft that are used for business rather than commercial airline purposes. The inclusion of types is somewhat arbitrary as many examples of the aircraft included are also flown by airlines for scheduled, charter or air taxi services.

All flying — other than military and airline — is known as General Aviation (GA). The primary purpose of aircraft included is to carry passengers between centres that are often off the scheduled airline map. In many instances these aircraft play an important role in Third World countries, where many governments run a kind of airline with small transports serving communities that have no proper surface communications.

A large percentage of aircraft covered in this category are operating in North America, but the number in Europe is growing year by year. The diversity of the aircraft illustrated — together with the numbers in use in early 1996 — show that manufacturers have been increasingly successful in selling their aircraft to business users. The book provides a recognition guide to the diverse types of aircraft operating in this field.

The aircraft are presented in the established 'Recognition Series' format, under the individual heading of the design company and/or principal manufacturer, followed by the aircraft's general descriptor. Standard headings are used to provide data on the aircraft's powerplant, dimensions and speed. Where known, the first flight date of the prototype is shown, followed by a broad outline of the aircraft's history, including an indication of the number of the type operating in this specialist category.

The key recognition features of the aircraft are then described. Photographs are shown with each type of aircraft to help with recognition. To assist in locating specific aircraft by name and/or manufacturer, a comprehensive index and cross reference has also been provided.

ACKNOWLEDGEMENTS

The author would particularly like to thank Robby Robinson and Brian Strickland for their assistance with the research, preparation and checking of the material, and Jean Strickland for typing the text.

Photographs

Most of the copyright illustrations in *abc Biz Jets: Business & Corporate Aircraft* are from the PRM Aviation Photo Library, as credited: Andrew March (APM), Daniel March (DJM), Peter R. March (PRM) and Brian Strickland (BSS). Additional photographs have been provided by Ben Dunnell, Peter Cooper, Mike Hooks and Mike Stroud.

Author

Peter R. March is also author of the following recent publications:
abc Civil Airliner Recognition (Ian Allan 1995)
abc Light Aircraft Recognition (Ian Allan 1995)
abc Classic & Warbird Recognition (Ian Allan 1996)
abc Military Aircraft Markings (Ian Allan 1996)
Royal Air Force Almanac (RAFBFE 1994)
Hawk Comes of Age (RAFBFE 1995)
The Real Aviation Enthusiast II (RAFBFE 1995)
and is Managing Editor of the *Royal Air Force Yearbook* series (RAF Benevolent Fund Enterprises).

Above:
BAC 1-11 475EZ. **PRM**

Below:
BAC 1-11 485 Ser 485. **DJM**

BAC 1-11

Twin turbofan short-range airliner and corporate transport
Data for: BAC 1-11 Series 400
Powerplant: Two 56kN (12,550lb st) Rolls-Royce Spey 512-14DW turbofans
Span: 28.50m (92ft 6in) *Length:* 32.61m (107ft 0in)
Max cruise speed: 871km/h (541mph)
Accommodation: 119 plus two crew
First aircraft flown: 20 August 1963

History: The BAC 1-11 had its origins in a project study by Hunting Aircraft that was working on a small jet airliner as early as 1956. As a jet successor to the turboprop Viscount it proved somewhat less successful than its illustrious forebear. The layout followed the style set by the Sud Caravelle, featuring a low wing with modest sweepback, a T-tail and engines on the rear fuselage. Series 200, 300 and 400 1-11s have a short fuselage, 28.50m (93ft 6in), and shorter span wings, 26.95m (88ft 8in), and are broadly the same externally in appearance. The larger Series 500 has a 4.14m (13ft 6in) longer fuselage and a 1.55m (5ft) extended wing span. The Series 475 has the short fuselage of the Series 400 and the bigger wings of the Series 500, together with a modified undercarriage with low pressure tyres and larger wheels. Internal rear air stairs make it independent of airport services. Some aircraft have been retrofitted with a large forward freight door; others have powerplant 'hush kits'. The first 67.24kN (15,100lb st) Tay 650 1-11 conversion was flown by Dee Howard in the USA in April 1990. Production:— 232 in UK (56 Series 200, nine Series 300, 69 Series 400, nine Series 475, 89 Series 500). Series 560 built by Romaero in Romania as the Rombac 1-11, the first aircraft being flown in September 1982; 16 on order at the end of 1995. In late 1995 there were 34 corporate BAC 1-11s flying (four 200 series; 29 400 series and one 500 series).

Recognition: Engines mounted either side of the rear fuselage forward of the tail unit. Slightly swept wings set in the lower section of the circular, narrow body fuselage. T-tailplane mounted on top of the swept fin and rudder. Auxiliary power unit (APU) in the tail cone.

Above:
Beechcraft 58 Baron. **PRM**

Below:
Beechcraft 95-B55 Baron. **PRM**

Beechcraft 55/56/58 Baron

Twin-engined light business and executive aircraft
Data for: Beechcraft 58P Baron
Powerplant: Two 242.5kW (325hp)
Continental TSIO-520-WB piston engines
Span: 11.53m (37ft 10in)
Length: 9.12m (29ft 11in)
Max cruise speed: 412km/h (256mph)
Accommodation: Pilot plus three/five passengers
First aircraft flown: 29 February 1960; 25 May

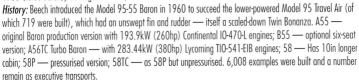

1966 (Turbo Baron); 16 August 1973 (Pressurised Baron)

History: Beech introduced the Model 95-55 Baron in 1960 to succeed the lower-powered Model 95 Travel Air (of which 719 were built), which had an unswept fin and rudder — itself a scaled-down Twin Bonanza. A55 — original Baron production version with 193.9kW (260hp) Continental IO-470-L engines; B55 — optional six-seat version; A56TC Turbo Baron — with 283.44kW (380hp) Lycoming TIO-541-EIB engines; 58 — Has 10in longer cabin; 58P — pressurised version; 58TC — as 58P but unpressurised. 6,008 examples were built and a number remain as executive transports.

Recognition: Twin-engined low-wing monoplane. Retractable tricycle undercarriage. Straight leading edge wing with square tips. Fairing at front wing root. Engines mounted high on wing leading edge. Swept fin and rudder with dorsal fairing from cabin. Three (some later models four) windows on each side. Tapered tailplane set low at fuselage extremity.

Above:
Beechcraft 60 Duke. **BSS**

Below:
Beechcraft 60 Duke. **PRM**

Beechcraft 60 Duke

Twin-engined light business and corporate aircraft
Data for: B60 Duke
Powerplant: Two 283.6kW (380hp) Lycoming
TIO-541-E1C4 turbocharged piston engines
Span: 11.97m (39ft 3in)
Length: 10.31m (33ft 10in)
Max cruise speed: 443km/h (275mph)
Accommodation: Pilot plus three/five passengers
First aircraft flown: 29 December 1966
History: Introduced in the late 1960s as a
pressurised, turbo-supercharged light transport to

complete the Beech twin-engined range. It fitted between the Baron light twin and the heavier family of Queen Airs. The 60 was the initial production version; the A60 had improved turbocharger and higher take-off weight and the B60, the main production version, had larger cabin and C90 pressurisation system. A total of 596 Dukes were built in three versions — the 60, A60 and B60 before production ceased.

Recognition: Low wings of equal taper and square tips. Fillet on leading edge of wing between fuselage sides and engine nacelles. Short, dumpy fuselage, with pronounced dorsal fin extending to the front window, a long pointed nose. Engines above and forward of wing. Three cabin windows each side. Swept fin and rudder. Swept tailplane, with dihedral mounted on top of pointed rear fuselage. Port side entry door.

Above:
Beechcraft 65-80 Queen Air. **DJM**

Below:
Beechcraft 65-80 Queen Air. **PRM**

Beechcraft 65/70/80 Queen Air

Twin-engined light business and corporate aircraft
Data for: 65 Queen Air
Powerplant: Two 253.7kW (340hp)
Lycoming ISGO-480-A1A6 piston engines
Span: 13.98m (45ft 10.5in)
Length: 10.82m (35ft 6in)
Max cruise speed: 344km/h (214 mph)
Accommodation: Pilot plus four/seven passengers
First aircraft flown: 28 August 1958

History: Introduced as a low-wing all-metal aircraft developed from the Model 50 Twin Bonanza with a new fuselage and tail. Like most of the Beech range, the Queen Air was built in very large numbers for both civil and military use. Military version known as L-23F (later U-8F/U-8G) Seminole. Model 65 initial model with upright tail; A65 — model 65 with swept vertical tail and fourth starboard cabin window; 70 — A65 with longer B80 wings and up to 11 seats; 65-80 — model 65 with 283.4kW (380hp) IGSO-540-A1A engines; 65-A80/B80 — longer span wing and 11/13 seats; 65-88 — A80 with 10-seat pressurised cabin and round porthole windows, powered by 283.4kW (380hp) IGSO-540-A1D; 89 Queen Airliner — an A80 for third level airlines. Total civil production was 1,004. Most surviving aircraft in use as corporate aircraft.

Recognition: Low wing with cranked leading edge. Small square tips. Long deep fuselage. Cabin windows usually square (but are oval on some versions). All have small oval window to rear of port entry door. Swept fin and rudder, with dorsal fillet. Tailplane, of equal taper and with slight dihedral, set midway on pointed rear fuselage.

Above:
Beechcraft 76 Duchess. **PRM**

Below:
Beechcraft 76 Duchess. PRM

Beechcraft 76 Duchess

Twin-engined light executive aircraft
Data for: Beechcraft 76 Duchess
Powerplant: Two 130.7kW (180hp)
Lycoming O-360-A1G6D piston engines
Span: 11.58m (38ft 0in)
Length: 8.86m (29ft 0in)
Max cruise speed: 308km/h (191mph)
Accommodation: Three passengers plus one crew
First aircraft flown: 24 May 1977

History: Beech developed the Model 76 from the single-engine Beechcraft 24R Sierra in the mid-1970s as an addition to its twin-engined range at the lighter end of the scale, to provide competition for the Cessna 310 and Piper Seneca. Following the adoption of a T-tail for the Super King Air 200, this same feature was used on the PD289, that first flew with 119.3kW (160hp) engines. Substituting higher powered engines, Beech decided to launch production of the new light twin as the Model 76 Duchess. A total of 437 were produced and many are in use as executive/corporate aircraft.

Recognition: Twin-engined low-wing monoplane with retractable tricycle undercarriage. Wings of parallel chord with square tips. Fairing at front wing root. Engines mounted high on wing leading edge. Swept oblong fin and rudder with dorsal fairing, square tips and T-tail. Three cabin windows on each side. Doors on both sides.

Above:
Corporate Boeing 707. **DJM**

Below:
Boeing 707-351C. **DJM**

Boeing 707/720

Four-turbofan medium/long-range transport
Data for: Boeing 720B
Powerplant: Four 75.7kN (17,000lb st)
Pratt & Whitney JT3D-1 turbofans
Span: 39.88m (130ft 10in)
Length: 41.88m (136ft 9in)
Max cruise speed: 978km/h (608mph)
Accommodation: Up to 167 plus three/four crew
First aircraft flown: 15 July 1954 (Boeing 707-80); 11 January 1959 (Boeing 707-320); 25 November 1959 (Boeing 720)

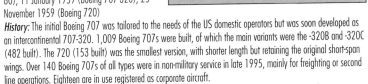

History: The initial Boeing 707 was tailored to the needs of the US domestic operators but was soon developed as an intercontinental 707-320. 1,009 Boeing 707s were built, of which the main variants were the -320B and -320C (482 built). The 720 (153 built) was the smallest version, with shorter length but retaining the original short-span wings. Over 140 Boeing 707s of all types were in non-military service in late 1995, mainly for freighting or second line operations. Eighteen are in use registered as corporate aircraft.

Recognition: Underwing-mounted engines in separate pods. Swept narrow chord wings low set. Circular, narrow body fuselage with the tailplane mounted either side of the tail cone. Tall, narrow fin and rudder, slightly swept and usually a small ventral fin.

Above:
Boeing 727-29C. **DJM**

Below:
Boeing 727-17. **PRM**

Boeing 727

Three-turbofan medium-range airliner and corporate transport
Data for: Boeing 727-200
Powerplant: Three 77.5kN (17,400lb st) Pratt & Whitney JT8D-17R turbofans
Span: 39.92m (108ft 0in)
Length: 49.69m (153ft 2in)
Max cruise speed: 964km/h (599mph)
Accommodation: 189 plus three crew
First aircraft flown: 9 February 1963 (Series 100); 30 December 1965 (727C)

History: The only rear-engined aircraft in the Boeing family, the 727 was the most widely sold of all Western jet airliners. A total of 1,831 built when production finished in August 1984, including 407 Series 100, 164 with large freight doors and 1,260 Series 200s and Advanced 200s. The original Series 100 was 10ft (3.05m) shorter than the Series 200 that was first flown on 27 July 1967. It also had more powerful engines and other improvements. The Advanced 200 has further powerplant and internal refinements. The first permanently re-engined Valsan 727-200s were marketed as Valsan 727. The 'Quiet 727' with higher-bypass Pratt & Whitney JT8D-217C in acoustically treated nacelles is in service with launch customers. Dee Howard is re-engineering up to 80 727-100s with Rolls-Royce Tay 651-54 turbofans, marketed as the 727-QF. In early 1996, 43 727-100s and 17 727-200s were used as corporate transports. Independence of airport services is ensured by an auxiliary power unit and ventral airstairs which makes it an ideal corporate aircraft.

Recognition: Three rear-mounted engines, one on top of fuselage at base and forward of fin, the other two in line either side of rear fuselage. Low-set swept wings midway along circular narrow-body fuselage. Swept fin and rudder with T-tailplane.

Above:
VIP Boeing 737-200. *via Mike Stroud*

Below:
Boeing 737-300. *APM*

Boeing 737-200/300/400/500

Twin-turbofan medium-range airliner and executive transport

Data for: Boeing 737-300
Powerplant: Two 97.86kN (22,000lb st) CFM International CFM56-3C-1 turbofans
Span: 28.88m (94ft 9in)
Length: 33.4m (109ft 7in)
Max cruise speed: 899km/h (558mph)
Accommodation: Varies according to model
First aircraft flown: 8 August 1967 (-200); 24 February 1984 (-300); 19 February 1988 (-400); 30 June 1989 (-500)
History: Design of this very successful short/medium-haul transport began in 1964. Introduced as the -100 series seating 115, it was subsequently increased to 130 in the 737-200. The -300 seats up to 149 passengers and the -400 up to 170. The shortened fuselage -500 (a combination of -300 and -400 technology) seats 108. The Executive has a typical layout for about 20 passengers, with conference room, bedroom, bathroom and full dining facilities. Registered as corporate aircraft are: Series 100 — 2; Series 200 — 25; Series 300 — 6; Series 400 — 1; Series 500 — 2. Series 100 had a 1.83m (6ft) shorter fuselage, but only 30 were built before the larger Series 200 entered service. The Series 300 has a 2.64m (8ft 8in) fuselage stretch; Series 400 has an increased length of 36.4m (119ft 7in) and Series 500 has a shortened fuselage of 31m (101ft 9in). The Series 700 is being developed to replace the similar sized -300 but with a new bigger wing and powered by 116.54kN (26,200lb st) CFM 56—7 engines and is due to enter service in 1997.
Recognition: The -200 has slim engines mounted directly under swept wing. The -300 and -400 differ from the -200 in wing span, fuselage length, outline and engine nacelle shape. The -500 has a shortened fuselage. Circular fuselage with wings set in the lower section. Tall, angular, slightly swept fin and rudder with pronounced dorsal fin. Swept tailplane set on rear fuselage at base of rudder.

11

Above:
Boeing 757-2J4. **PRM**

Boeing 757

Twin-turbofan short/medium/extended-range airliner and corporate transport
Data for: Boeing 757-200 Corporate
Powerplant: Two 178kN (40,100lb st) Rolls-Royce RB211-535E4 or P&W 170kN (38,200lb st) PW2037 turbofans
Span: 38.05m (124ft 10in)
Length: 47.32m (155ft 3in)
Max cruise speed: 916km/h (569mph)
Accommodation: 239 plus two crew
First aircraft flown: 19 February 1982
History: Reversing the trend towards wide-body twin-aisle transports, the slim-body, with two large turbofans, single-aisle, and new technology Boeing 757 was introduced in the early 1980s. Operators had a choice of powerplants, most selecting either Rolls-Royce or Pratt & Whitney. The Boeing 757-200F freighter has a forward cargo door and a windowless fuselage. The 757-200M Combi has a forward port cargo door and carries up to 150 passengers. The 757-200ER is the extended range version. Six 757s are in use as corporate transports — four in the USA, one in Europe and one in Asia.
Recognition: Engines in nacelles under wings. Very long, circular, narrow-body fuselage with swept, low-set wings at midway point, giving appearance of very long nose. Pronounced lower fuselage bulge for undercarriage fairing. Tall, swept fin and rudder with swept tailplane on either side of rear fuselage below fin.

Above:
Canadair CL601-3R Challenger. ***APM***

Canadair CL600/601-3A Challenger
Twin-turbofan business, regional and corporate transport
Data for: Challenger 601-3A
Powerplant: Two 40.66kN (9,140lb st) General Electric CF34-3A turbofans
Span: 19.61m (64ft 4in) (over winglets)
Length: 20.85m (68ft 5in)
Max cruise speed: 882km/h (548mph)
Accommodation: 19 passengers plus two crew
First aircraft flown: 8 November 1978 (Challenger 600); 28 September 1986 (601-3A); 8 November 1988 (601-3A-ER)
History: In the mid-1970s, Canadair became involved in the Learstar 600 business jet that was designed by Bill Lear. Canadair obtained rights to the Learstar in 1976 and undertook extensive redesign including a T-tail configuration, which became the Challenger two years later. Challenger 601-1A, first production version (first flew 17 September 1982), with 66 built. Challenger 601-3A — current production aircraft with 'glass cockpit' and upgraded CF34s. Challenger 601-3A/ER is an extended range version that first flew on 8 November 1988. CL-601S — a 3A with reduced interior and avionics specification and lower fuel capacity. CL-601-3R — a 3A with CF34-3AL engines, enlarged fuel capacity, new environmental control system and new cabin windows. CL-604 — development of CL-601-3R with increased fuel tanks and range, revised undercarriage, new underbelly fairing, larger cabin, new avionics and CF34-3B engines — first flew on 18 September 1994. A corporate version with a 30-passenger interior as the Canadair Corporate Jetliner was launched in November 1991. Currently 71 600s, 54 601s, 195 601-3A/3Rs and two 604s are registered to corporate owners.
Recognition: Low-set swept wings, with winglets, mounted midway along fuselage. Circular fuselage, with streamlined windscreen. Swept tail and T-tail. Small APU housing at front base of fin. Twin large diameter engines set high on each side of rear fuselage, with pronounced pointed exhaust cones, with fairing between engine and cone. Six oblong windows on each side. Front entry door on port side.

Above:
Canadair CL601-3R Challenger. DJM

Below:
Canadair CL601-3R Challenger. **PRM**

Above:
CASA C-212 Series 300 Aviocar. via **M. J. Hooks**

Below:
CASA C-212 Series 300 Aviocar. **M. J. Hooks**

CASA C-212 Aviocar

Twin-turboprop commuter airliner and light/corporate transport
Data for: C-212-300 Aviocar
Powerplant: Two 671kW (900shp) Garrett TPE331-10R-513C turboprops
Span: 20.28m (66ft 61.5in)
Length: 16.15m (52ft 11.75in)
Max cruise speed: 354km/h (220mph)
Accommodation: 23/26 plus one/two crew

First aircraft flown: 26 March 1971 (Series 200); September 1984 (Series 300)
History: The Aviocar was designed initially to meet Spanish Air Force requirements for a multi-role transport, with potential for later development in civil guise. The initial production Series 100 had lower power turboprops; the Series 200 is externally similar. The latest Series 300 features a larger cabin, bigger baggage compartment, better sound-proofing and improved aerodynamics. Over 500 sold in 35 countries for civil and military use, including about a quarter built under licence by Nurtania in Indonesia. CASA produces a corporate version of the 26-seat C-212 Series 300 Aviocar. Corporate versions delivered by early 1996: 212-100 — three; 212-200 — five.
Recognition: Twin turboprops mounted forward of high, straight wing, with winglets. A rectangular fuselage with short, pointed nose and upswept rear section. An angular fin and rudder with large dorsal extension. Undercarriage fairings on lower fuselage below wing. Tailplane positioned below fin and rudder on extension of fuselage.

Above:
Cessna 208B Grand Caravan. **PRM**

Below:
Cessna 208B Grand Caravan. **PRM**

Cessna 208 Caravan I

Single-turboprop civil, military multi-mission and corporate aircraft
Data for: Caravan I — Model 208A
Powerplant: One 447kW (600shp)
Pratt & Whitney Canada PT6A-114 turboprop
Span: 15.88m (52ft 1in)
Length: 11.46m (37ft 7in)
Max cruise speed: 341km/h (212mph)
Accommodation: Up to 14 passengers plus one crew
First aircraft flown: 9 December 1982 (208A); 3 March 1986 (208B)
History: After the crisis in the mid-1980s over product liability Cessna suspended production of all small aircraft and concentrated on the Citation and Caravan I. Production: 208 Caravan I — 61; 208A Cargomaster — 177; 208B Super Cargomaster — 404; 208B Grand Caravan — production continuing. A large all-metal high-wing utility aircraft with fixed tricycle undercarriage and four doors — including port side double door. Model 208A Cargomaster — basic utility model featuring a windowless fuselage for passengers or cargo. Commissioned by Federal Express Corporation as Cargomaster freighter with an underfuselage cargo pannier. Model 208B — stretched version, developed at request of Federal Express and commissioned as Super Cargomaster. U-27A is the military utility/special mission derivative of 208A and 208B versions of Caravan I with large roller-blind door. The 208A is available as an amphibian, using Wipline floats. Over 650 are in service, many with corporate users. Federal Express purchased 100 Model 208As and 70 Model 208Bs.
Recognition: High-mounted wing with single supporting strut on either side from base of fuselage. Wings of equal taper with square tips. Non-retractable tricycle type undercarriage, with single wheel on each unit. Forward hinged door for pilot. Main door on port side at rear. Six windows on each side of fuselage. Amphibian has small additional fins on tailplane. Cargomaster has ventral fuselage pannier.

Above:
Cessna 340A. **PRM**

Below:
Cessna 340A. **PRM**

Cessna 340A

Four-passenger pressurised business
and corporate aircraft
Data for: Cessna 340A
Powerplant: Two 231.2kW (310hp)
Continental TSIO-520-N flat-four piston engines
Span: 11.62m (38ft 1in)
Length: 10.46m (34ft 4in)
Max cruise speed: 448km/h (278mph)
Accommodation: Four passengers plus two crew

First aircraft flown: 310 — 3 January 1953; 340 — 1971

History: A low-wing six-seat pressurised light twin based on the Cessna 330 with retractable undercarriage. Production: 340 — 350; 340A — 948. 340 was the original version with 212.5kW (285hp) Continental TSIO-520-K engines. The 340A has better air conditioning, new seating, increased take-off weight, propeller synchrophasers and the higher powered engines. A considerable number are registered to corporate users.

Recognition: Low wing with straight leading edge and tip tanks. Twin-engines in shallow cowlings mainly on top of wing, with small nacelle protruding behind trailing edge. Sharply pointed nose, raked windscreen. Four oval windows on each side of fuselage. Port entry door at rear. Swept fin and rudder with small dorsal fillet. Tailplane, of equal taper, set at fuselage extremity. Slim ventral strake at rear.

Above:
Cessna 402C II. ***PRM***

Right:
Cessna 414 Chancellor II. ***PRM***

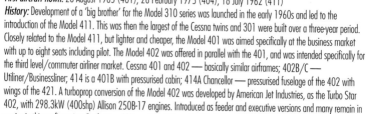

Cessna 401/402/411/414
Twin-engined business, air taxi and corporate aircraft
Data for: Cessna 402C
Powerplant: Two 240kW (325hp) Continental TSIO-520-VB turbo-supercharged piston engines
Span: 13.45m (44ft 2in)   *Length:* 11.09m (36ft 4in)
Max cruise speed: 394km/h (245mph)   *Accommodation:* Pilot plus five/seven passengers
First aircraft flown: 26 August 1965 (401); 26 February 1975 (404); 18 July 1962 (411)
History: Development of a 'big brother' for the Model 310 series was launched in the early 1960s and led to the introduction of the Model 411. This was then the largest of the Cessna twins and 301 were built over a three-year period. Closely related to the Model 411, but lighter and cheaper, the Model 401 was aimed specifically at the business market with up to eight seats including pilot. The Model 402 was offered in parallel with the 401, and was intended specifically for the third level/commuter airliner market. Cessna 401 and 402 — basically similar airframes; 402B/C — Utiliner/Businessliner; 414 is a 401B with pressurised cabin; 414A Chancellor — pressurised fuselage of the 402 with wings of the 421. A turboprop conversion of the Model 402 was developed by American Jet Industries, as the Turbo Star 402, with 298.3kW (400shp) Allison 250B-17 engines. Introduced as feeder and executive versions and many remain in service in this configuration. Production: 401 — 54; 402 — 1,645; 404 — 396; 411 — 302; 414 — 516; 414A — 554. Many are used as corporate aircraft.
Recognition: Low-wing twin-engined monoplane. Straight leading edge to wings and wing tip tanks. Swept fin and rudder with dorsal fillet forward of fin. Engine nacelles protrude behind wings. 401 models had oval windows whereas 402/404/406 featured square-edged side windows.

Above:
Cessna 421C Golden Eagle III. **PRM**

Right:
Cessna 441 Conquest II. **PRM**

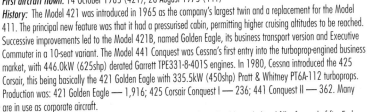

Cessna 421 Golden Eagle/ 425 Corsair/Conquest I/441 Conquest II

Twin-engined business, commuter and executive aircraft
Data for: Cessna 421B Golden Eagle
Powerplant: Two 279.8kW (375hp)
Continental GTSIO-520-N turbo-supercharged piston engines
Span: 12.53m (41ft 2in) *Length:* 11.09m (36ft 4in)
Max cruise speed: 447km/h (278mph) *Accommodation:* Pilot plus five/ten passengers
First aircraft flown: 14 October 1965 (421); 26 August 1975 (441)
History: The Model 421 was introduced in 1965 as the company's largest twin and a replacement for the Model 411. The principal new feature was that it had a pressurised cabin, permitting higher cruising altitudes to be reached. Successive improvements led to the Model 421B, named Golden Eagle, its business transport version and Executive Commuter in a 10-seat variant. The Model 441 Conquest was Cessna's first entry into the turboprop-engined business market, with 446.0kW (625shp) derated Garrett TPE331-8-401S engines. In 1980, Cessna introduced the 425 Corsair, this being basically the 421 Golden Eagle with 335.5kW (450shp) Pratt & Whitney PT6A-112 turboprops. Production was: 421 Golden Eagle — 1,916; 425 Corsair Conquest I — 236; 441 Conquest II — 362. Many are in use as corporate aircraft.
Recognition: Low-wing twin-engined monoplane. Single swept fin and rudder with dorsal fillet forward of fin. Early versions have wing tip tanks. All models feature oval windows, varying in number according to model.

Above:
Cessna 500 Citation I. *PRM*

Below:
Cessna 500 Citation I. *PRM*

Cessna 500/501 Citation I

Six-passenger twin-turbofan business and
corporate jet
Data for: Model 501
Powerplant: Two 9.79kN (2,200lb st) Pratt &
Whitney Canada JT15D-1A turbofans
Span: 14.36m (47ft 1in)
Length: 13.27m (43ft 6in)
Max cruise speed: 650km/h (404mph)
Accommodation: Six passengers plus two crew

First aircraft flown: 15 September 1969 (Citation 500); 1976 (Citation 501)
History: Introduced by Cessna as an eight-seat business jet powered by turbofans. Initially known as the Fanjet 500,
the company's first business jet, the name was changed to Model 500 Citation. A switch was then made to the
improved Model 501 Citation I which has uprated engines and an increase of 2.21m (7ft 3in) wing span. A single-
pilot operation, mainly for pilot training aircraft by airlines, is known as the Citation I/SP. Currently 390 Citation I and
321 Citation I/SP are registered to corporate owners.
Recognition: Low wing, with straight leading edge and square tips mounted well back on fuselage. Large windscreen
area to cockpit. Four windows on each side of fuselage. Engines pod-mounted high on each side of rear fuselage,
with intake just ahead of trailing edge of wing. Swept fin and rudder with dorsal fillet. Tailplane of equal taper has
noticeable dihedral and is set half-way up the fin.

Above:
Cessna 525 CitationJet. ***PRM***

Cessna 525 CitationJet

Twin-turbofan business and corporate jet
Data for: CitationJet
Powerplants: Two 8.45kN (1,900lb st) Rolls-Royce/Williams International FJ44 turbofans
Span: 13.78m (45ft 2.4in)
Length: 12.98m (42ft 7.25in)
Max cruise speed: 704km/h (438mph)
Accommodation: Five passengers plus one crew
First aircraft flown: 29 April 1991
History: The CitationJet was built to replace the Citation 500 and I (production of which stopped in 1985). It received certification for single-pilot operation in 1991. Compared with the Citation I, the CitationJet has a fuselage shortened by 0.27m (10.75in) and wing span reduced by 0.57m (1ft 10.5in). The cabin height has been increased by 13cm (5in) by the lowering of the centre aisle. A new supercritical laminar-flow wing aerofoil and a high T-tail have been incorporated. With a VIP configuration of one crew and four passengers it has a range of 2,780km (1,727 miles). In early 1996, 13 CitationJets were registered to corporate users.
Recognition: Straight leading edge to wing, low mounted with a slight bulge under central fuselage. Swept fin and rudder. Angular T-tail. Two large diameter engines pod-mounted high on sides of rear fuselage. Short, squat fuselage. Large

Above:
Cessna 551 Citation II. *via PRM*

Below:
Cessna 550 Citation II. *PRM*

glazed area to cockpit. Four oblong cabin windows. Entry door at front on port side. Very short legged undercarriage.

Cessna 550/551 Citation II

Six/ten passenger twin-turbofan business and corporate jet
Data for: Citation II
Powerplant: Two 11.12kN (2,500lb st)
Pratt & Whitney JT15D-4B turbofans
Span: 15.76m (51ft 8.5in)
Length: 14.39m (47ft 2.5in)
Max cruise speed: 468km/h (302mph)
Accommodation: Six/ten passengers plus one crew
First aircraft flown: 31 January 1977
History: Basically a stretched Citation I with up to 12 seats and six cabin-windows. 587 Citation IIs were delivered had been phased out in favour of Citation S/II in 1984 — but production resumed in 1985. The Model 550 Citation II was the first version for single-pilot operation; Model 551 Citation II/SP is for single-pilot operation. Model S550 Citation S/II is a six/eight-passenger improved Citation II, with new wing aerofoil, that first flew on 14 February 1984. The Model 552 is the T-47A, of which 15 were acquired by the US Navy for the radar training role. The 550B Citation Bravo is a Citation II with two 12.24kN (2,750lb st) Pratt & Whitney PW530A turbofans with thrust reversers, longer range, improved short field performance and airstair door. 455 Citation II and 113 IIPs are registered to corporate users.
Recognition: Cranked leading edge to low-mounted straight wing. Long pointed nose with large glazed cockpit

Above:
Cessna 560 Citation V. **PRM**

Below:
Cessna 560 Citation V. **PRM**

Cessna 560 Citation V

Twin-turbofan business and corporate jet
Data for: Citation V
Powerplant: Two 12.89kN (2,900lb st) Pratt & Whitney Canada JT15D-5A turbofans
Span: 15.90m (52ft 2.5in)
Length: 14.90m (48ft 10.75in)
Max cruise speed: 791km/h (492mph)
Accommodation: Eight passengers plus one crew
First aircraft flown: August 1987 (Citation V); February 1991 (Citation VII)

History: The Citation V is a stretched
Citation S/II with seven cabin windows
on each side. Citation Excel is a proposed
new design with Citation V wings and
tail, shortened Citation III fuselage and
two Pratt & Whitney PW545A turbofans.
Currently there are 380 Citation Vs
registered to corporate users.
Recognition: A stretched version of the
Citation III. Cranked leading edge to low-
mounted straight wing. Long pointed
nose with large glazed cockpit canopy.

Seven windows on each side, forward door on port side. Swept tail with pronounced fillet at front base. Dihedralled
tailplane set half-way up the fin.

Above:
Cessna 650 Citation III. **PRM**

Below:
Cessna 650 Citation VII. **PRM**

Cessna 650 Citation III, VI, VII and X

Six/thirteen-seat high-speed long-range executive jet transport
Data for: Citation III
Powerplant: Two 16.25kN (3,650lb st)
Garrett TFE731-3B-100S turbofans
Span: 16.3m (53ft 4in)
Length: 16.8m (55ft 2.5in)
Max cruise speed: 869km/h (540mph)
Accommodation: Six passengers plus two crew
First aircraft flown: 30 May 1979 (Citation III); December 1993 (Citation X)
History: Introduced as an 8/9-seat low-wing intercontinental business jet. The wings are in one piece which improves the headroom in the cabin. Production ended late 1991. Total deliveries — 201, including 12 in 1991. Superseded by Citation VI and VII. The Model 750 Citation X, with two 26.69kN (6,000lb st) Allison AE3007 turbofans, is the latest model with the forward fuselage/cockpit section derived from the Citation VI. First flew in December 1993 and able to fly at Mach 0.92 with a range of 3,300nm. The Model 650 Citation VI is a six/nine-passenger jet, simplified, lower-cost version of the Citation III with standard systems package. The top range Citation X has a bigger cabin than a normal mid-sized jet with a new generation engine for fuel efficiency. The Citation VII is a more powerful version of the Citation III fitted with two 17.79kN (4,000lb st) Garrett TFE731-4R-2S turbofans for improved 'hot and high' performance. Engines pod-mounted on sides of rear fuselage. Very short tricycle undercarriage. 196 Citation IIIs, 37 VIs, 65 VIIIs and 3 Xs are currently registered to corporate users.
Recognition: High aspect ratio swept wing and T-tail. Pod-mounted engines on sides of rear fuselage. Swept fin and rudder with dorsal fillet. Swept tailplane, with no dihedral, set half-way up the fin. No ventral strake. Six windows on each side of fuselage. Port entry door at front.

Above:
Cessna 404 Titan. **Ben Dunnell**

Below:
Cessna 404 Titan. **PRM**

Cessna Titan

Twin-engined business and corporate aircraft
Data for: Model 404 Titan
Powerplant: Two 279.6kW (375hp) Continental
GTSIO-520-M turbo-supercharged flat-six piston engines
Span: 14.12m (46ft 4in)
Length: 12.04m (39ft 5in)
Max cruise speed: 369km/h (229mph)
Accommodation: Up to 10, including pilot
First aircraft flown: 26 February 1975

History: Now the largest of the piston-engined twin built by Cessna, offered as the Model 404 in versions equipped specifically for the needs of the businessman and of the third level/commuter airlines. Similar in general size and characteristics to the Model 421, but without cabin pressurisation. Its wing and landing gear are substantially the same as those of the Model 441 Conquest — but the fuselage was new, offering more capacity than available in the Model 402. A large cargo door was available as an option, permitting the loading of freight containers or items of unusual size. The Model 404 designation was subsequently dropped and the Titan was offered in three versions — the Ambassador for the business/executive market, the Courier for the commuter and the Freighter for cargo operations. A large number of the 396 built are used as corporate aircraft.

Recognition: Low-wing twin-engined monoplane. Single swept fin and rudder with dorsal fillet forward of fin. Straight leading edge to wing, with square tips. Engine nacelles protrude behind wings. Double cargo door on port side, above wing trailing edge. Dihedral tailplane set low on rear fuselage. Seven cabin windows, of varying sizes on each side of fuselage.

Above:
Commander 114. **PRM**

Below:
Commander 114. **PRM**

Commander 112/114

Single-engined four-seat light and corporate aircraft
Data for: Commander 114
Powerplant: 193.9kW (260hp) Lycoming IO-540-T4B5D
piston engine
Span: 10.85m (35ft 7in)
Length: 7.62m (25ft 0in)
Max cruise speed: 291km/h (181mph)
Accommodation: Pilot plus three passengers
First aircraft flown: 4 December 1970 (112); 1976 (114)

History: The four-seat, single-engined Aero Commander Model 112 was the first of an entirely new range of light aircraft utilising many common components. The 112 is powered by a 149.1kW (200hp) Lycoming IO-360-C1D6 engine and was introduced to compete with existing light aircraft from the Piper Cherokee to the Beech Bonanza. Commander Air is the current manufacturer. 112A — structurally strengthened model; 112B — 34in wing span increase, larger wheels; 112TC — turbocharged version with 156.6kW (210hp) Lycoming TIO-360-C1A6D engine; 114 — with 260hp engine; 114A — Gran Turismo model; 114B — the new model when production restarted in 1992; 114AT — a trainer version introduced mid-1994 and 114TC introduced in 1995. Total production to end of 1995 was: 112 - 801; 114 — 520+ and a small number are used as corporate aircraft.

Recognition: Low-wing monoplane with retractable tricycle undercarriage. Straight leading edge to wing with fairing at front root. Tapered trailing edge with square tips. Large swept fin and rudder with dorsal fairing from cabin. Very small ventral strake. Twin side windows. Tapered tailplane set half-way up the fin

Above:
Dassault Falcon 20F-5.
PRM

Right:
Dassault Falcon 2000. DJM

Dassault Mystère/Falcon 20/200/2000

Twin-engined business and corporate jet transport
Data for: Falcon 20F
Powerplant: Two 20.04kN (4,500lb st)
General Electric CF700-2D-2 turbofans
Span: 16.30m (53ft 6in) *Length:* 17.15m (56ft 3in)
Max cruise speed: 862km/h (536mph) *Accommodation:* Nine passengers plus two crew
First aircraft flown: 4 May 1963 (Mystère XX); 20 February 1970 (Falcon 20F);
28 November 1977 (Falcon 20G); 3 March 1993 (Falcon 2000)
History: Introduced as a business jet with intercontinental range. Production: Falcon 20C — 166; Falcon 20CC — 1; Falcon 20D — 86; Falcon 20E — 60; Falcon 20F — 134; Falcon 20G — 47; Falcon 20H — 1; Falcon 200 — 36. The last of the Falcon 20 series was completed in mid-1990. Originally known as the Mystère 20 executive jet in France. The aircraft is known in the USA, and generally outside of France, as the Falcon 20. The standard Falcon was followed by the C, D, E and F versions, the latest having upgraded engines, more fuel, new high-lift devices and other improvements. Four aircraft, designated Falcon STs, had Mirage combat radar and navigation installations for the French Air Force. Falcon D Cargo Jets were developed by Little Rock Airmotive for Federal Express Corporation. Another prolific version was the Falcon 20G Guardian for maritime surveillance — 41 being acquired by the US Coast Guard (HU-25A). The Falcon 2000 is a follow-on to the 20/200 — 12 passengers and fitted with two 26.7kN (6,000lb st) GE/Garrett CFE738 turbofans. Currently there are 387 Falcon 20 series and 23 Falcon 2000s registered to corporate concerns.
Recognition: Swept wings low-mounted half-way along under fuselage. Engines pod-mounted on each side of rear fuselage. Five oval windows on each side. Raked windscreen. Large swept fin and rudder. Swept tailplane set half-way up fin. Pronounced wing-fence on each wing.

Above:
Dassault Falcon 50. **PRM**

Below:
Dassault Falcon 50. **PRM**

Above:
Dassault Falcon 50. ***PRM***

Dassault Falcon 50

Three-turbofan long-range business and corporate transport
Data for: Falcon 50
Powerplant: Three 16.5kN (3,700lb st) Garrett TFE731-3 turbofans
Span: 18.86m (61ft 10.5in)
Length: 18.43m (60ft 5.75in)
Max cruise speed: 880km/h (546mph)
Accommodation: Ten passengers plus two/three crew
First aircraft flown: 7 November 1976
History: Introduced as a 10/12-seat intercontinental business jet based on the Falcon 20 with the same cross-section but longer fuselage and seven windows on each side. Powered by three turbofans. A total of 245 were sold to 30 countries between July 1979 and 31 December 1991. Currently there are 144 Falcon 50s registered as corporate aircraft.
Recognition: Two engines pod-mounted on sides of rear fuselage, the third attached on top of rear fuselage exhausting through tail cone. Swept wings have compound leading edge sweep and optimised section. Circular section fuselage is sharply waisted at the rear. Wings low-mounted in slight bulge under central fuselage. Swept tail fin and swept tailplane (with slight anhedral) set half-way up fin.

Above:
Dassault Falcon 900. AMD-BA/Aviaplans

Below:
Dassault Falcon 900. **PRM**

Dassault Falcon 900

Three-turbofan intercontinental business and corporate transport

Data for: Falcon 900B
Powerplant: Three 21.13kN (4,750lb st) Garrett TFE731-5B turbofans
Span: 19.33m (63ft 5in)
Length: 20.21m (66ft 3.75in)
Max cruise speed: 927km/h (575mph)
Accommodation: 19 passengers plus two crew
First aircraft flown: 21 September 1984
History: A scaled-up development of the Falcon 50

with a typical 13-passenger luxury interior or 36-seat high density cabin. Production of Falcon 900 — 150 plus; Falcon 900B — production continuing. The Falcon 900 was the original standard version; the Falcon 900B was certified in 1991, with uprated engines and increased speed range. Falcon 900EX, a development of the 900B with additional fuel and range, is powered by three 22.26kN (5,000lb st) TFE738 turbofans and first flew in May 1995. Currently 147 Falcon 900s are registered as corporate aircraft.

Recognition: Larger cross-section circular fuselage and cabin length than Falcon 50. Wing optimised for Mach 0.54 cruise. Quarter-chord sweepback on outer wings. Carbon fibre central cowling around all three engines. Two engines pod-mounted on sides of rear fuselage, the third attached by two top mounts. Wings low-mounted in slight bulge under central fuselage. Swept tail fin and swept tailplane (with slight anhedral) set half-way up fin.

Above:
De Havilland DHC-6 Twin Otter. **APM**

Below:
De Havilland DHC-6 Twin Otter. **APM**

De Havilland DHC-6 Twin Otter

General purpose STOL commuter airliner and
corporate transport
Data for: Twin Otter Series 300S
Powerplant: Two 486.2kW (652shp)
Pratt & Whitney Canada PT6A-27 turboprops
Span: 19.81m (65ft 0in)
Length: 15.77m (51ft 9in)
Max cruise speed: 338km/h (210mph)
Accommodation: Up to 20 passengers plus pilot
First aircraft flown: 20 May 1965

History: First announced in 1964, the Twin Otter was
derived from the single-engined Otter, produced as a general purpose and military STOL transport, able to operate from short
rough fields. It took on many roles including services with Antarctic expeditions. The last Twin Otter was completed in
December 1988 following a production run of 844 — a large percentage going for export. The initial model was the
Series 100 with 431kW (578shp) PT6A-20 engines and a short nose. This was replaced by the Series 200 in April 1968
with a lengthened nose. Floatplanes have been produced, all having the short nose. The Series 300 is similar but with
larger engines. Produced for the Canadian Forces as CC-138 and US Army as UV-18A. The 300S has added safety features.
Some 37 are currently registered worldwide as business aircraft.

Recognition: Strut-braced high-wing monoplane with a fixed tricycle undercarriage. Floatplane versions have short nose and
small additional fins above and below the tailplane. Straight wings of equal chord. Large, slightly swept fin and rudder, with
oblong tailplane mounted half-way up fin. Seven cabin windows on each side with large entry door at rear of port side.

31

Above:
Dornier 328. **PRM**

Below:
Dornier 328. DJM

Dornier 328

Twin-turboprop commuter airliner and corporate transport
Data for: Dornier 328
Powerplant: Two 1,625kW (2,180shp) Pratt & Whitney Canada PW119B turboprops
Span: 20.98m (68ft 10in)   *Length:* 21.28m (69ft 7.5in)
Max cruise speed: 620km/h (388mph)
Accommodation: 30/33 plus two crew
First aircraft flown: 6 December 1991
History: The Dornier 328 combines the basic supercritical wing of the Do228 with a new pressurised fuselage. The internal volume was designed to give passengers more seat width than in a Boeing 727 or 737 and stand-up

headroom. The Dornier 328S is a high speed 40/69-passenger regional turboprop stretched version (6.8m — 22ft 3.75in longer). In early 1996 four Dornier 328s were registered as corporate aircraft.

Recognition: Small turboprops mounted on the leading edge of the 'new technology' wing with pointed tips. Six-blade propellers. Circular fuselage positioned below high, shoulder wing. Swept fin and rudder with small T-tail and pointed rear fuselage cone. Twin ventral strakes. The main undercarriage retracts into lower fuselage fairing.

Above:
Douglas DC-3. **PRM**

Below:
Douglas DC-3. **PRM**

Douglas DC-3 Dakota

Twin piston-engined short-range transport
and corporate aircraft

Data for: Douglas DC-3
Powerplant: Two 895kW (1,200hp) Pratt & Whitney
R-1830-92 Twin Wasp radial piston engines
Span: 28.96m (95ft 0in)
Length: 19.66m (64ft 6in)
Max cruise speed: 312km/h (194mph)
Accommodation: 32 plus two crew
First aircraft flown: 17 December 1935
History: The most widely used air transport in history. It began life as the 14-passenger Douglas DST and developed via the DC-1 to the DC-2 and then the DC-3. During World War 2 10,225 DC-3s were built and many were subsequently converted for civil use. Various modifications have been made to the DC-3 for VIP use with modified windows, powerplant refinements, nose radar and fully enclosed housings for the main wheels; cargo versions feature large 'double' doors on the port side of the rear fuselage. Of the total built, only 458 were originally for civilian use. Some 450 remain in commercial use today and a number are operated as corporate aircraft.
Recognition: Engines are positioned forward of wing, close to fuselage. A low-set wing with swept leading edges and dihedral outboard of engines, straight trailing edge and almost pointed wing tips. Oval fuselage set above wing with distinctive rounded nose. Broad fin and rudder with curved top. Mounted on either side of fuselage below fin, tailplane has swept front edge and straight trailing edge. Main undercarriage retracts into lower part of engine cowlings leaving one-third of wheel exposed; non-retracting tailwheel.

Above:
Embraer EMB-120 Brasilia. **PRM**

Below:
Embraer EMB-120 Brasilia. **APM**

Embraer EMB-120 Brasilia

Twin-turboprop regional airliner and corporate transport
Data for: EMB-120ER
Powerplant: Two 1,341kW (1,800shp) Pratt & Whitney
Canada PW118A turboprops
Span: 19.78m (64ft 10.75in)
Length: 18.73m (61ft 5.5in)
Max cruise speed: 555km/h (345mph)
Accommodation: 30 with two crew
First aircraft flown: 27 July 1983

History: Production of the Bandeirante and Xingu was completed in the 1980s and was succeeded by the EMB-120
Brasilia local service airliner. First delivery to US commuter airlines in July 1985 and DLT in Germany in January
1986. The state-owned Brazilian aircraft manufacturer was privatised in December 1994. The company has
upgraded the Brasilia to a new -120ERX specification which is the standard to which corporate aircraft and regional
airliners are now built. A 'hot and high' version with reduced structural weight and more powerful PW118A
turboprops was launched in 1988. The EMB-145 Amazon with Allison GMA3007 turbofans is based on the Brasilia
fuselage. It will carry up to 50 passengers and flew in mid-1995, with deliveries in late 1996. Embraer hopes to
launch its 50-seat EMB-145 regional jet in corporate form during 1996. Corporate versions at early 1996 are: EMB-
110 — 30; EMB-120 — one; EMB-121 — 45 and EMB-121-2 — 10.

Recognition: Two turboprops projecting forward from the low-set, straight wings. Wings have a slight dihedral, and
leading edge is swept inboard of engines. Slim, circular fuselage with large swept fin and rudder with dorsal
projection. The swept tailplane is located on top of fin. Pointed nose with sharply raked large cockpit windscreens.

Above:
Swearingen Merlin IIB. **PRM**

Below:
Swearingen Merlin III. **PRM**

Fairchild-Swearingen SA-225T Merlin II/III

Twin-turboprop corporate/business aircraft
Data for: Merlin III
Powerplant: Two 626.3kW (840shp) Garrett AiResearch
TPE331-3U-303G turboprops
Span: 14.10m (46ft 3in)
Length: 12.85m (42ft 2in)
Max cruise speed: 523km/h (325mph)
Accommodation: Six/eight plus two crew
First aircraft flown: 1970

History: The Swearingen range of business twins derives from
the original specialised conversion (designed by Ed Swearingen) making use of Beech Queen Air wings and engines,
Twin Bonanza undercarriage and a new pressurised fuselage. With turboprop engines replacing the piston engines,
these evolved into the Merlin IIA and Merlin IIB. The Merlin III is a substantially altered IIB with a new fuselage, new
tailplane position, uprated engines, taller undercarriage and other improvements. In early 1996 there were eight
Merlin IIAs, 65 Merlin IIBs and 158 Merlin IIIs registered to corporate users.

Recognition: Low-wing twin-engined monoplane. Wings of equal taper with small square tips. Engines mounted well
ahead of leading edge of wing. Slightly swept tail fin with pronounced dorsal fillet. Steeply swept tailplane —
mounted low on the II but half-way up the fin on the III. Three large square cabin windows on each side of fuselage.
Small ventral strake at rear (III). Port entry door at rear.

Above:
Fairchild Metro 23. via **PRM**

Below:
Fairchild Metro 23. BSS

Fairchild-Swearingen Metro III/23
Twin-turboprop commuter airliner and corporate transport
Data for: Metro III
Powerplant: Two 820kW (1,100shp)
Garrett TPE331-12UAR turboprops
Span: 17.37m (57ft 0in)
Length: 18.09m (59ft 4.25in)
Max cruise speed: 511km/h (317mph)
Accommodation: 19 plus two crew
First aircraft flown: 26 August 1969

History: Originally developed by Swearingen as the Merlin, the pressurised Metro was built by Fairchild. The Metro II had the Merlin's nose and tail, with a new and much longer, round section, pressurised fuselage, with larger windows and other refinements. The Metro III features a new wing of 3.28m (10ft 9in) greater span; the Expediter is an all-cargo version with a strengthened cabin floor. The Merlin IVC is a corporate version and the C-26A is a variant for the US Air National Guard. The 19-passenger Metro V, with TPE331-12s, is Fairchild's successor to the Metro III and includes a 'stand-up' cabin. The Metro 23 is an increased max take-off variant. Over 900 of all variants delivered by late-1995, including 20 Expediters. A small number are in corporate use.

Recognition: A long, slender, circular section fuselage is mounted above slightly tapered wings. Twin turboprops extend well forward of wings and are close into fuselage. Raked fin and rudder seem small on the longer fuselage which appears to have wings set too far forward. Tailplane, set above fuselage on dorsal extension, is swept sharply.

Above:
Fokker F27-200 Friendship. ***PRM***

Fokker F27 Friendship/Fairchild FH227

Twin-turboprop short-range transport and corporate aircraft
Data for: F27 Mk 500 Friendship
Powerplant: Two 1,730kW (2,320shp) Rolls-Royce Dart 536-7R turboprops
Span: 29.01m (95ft 2in)
Length: 25.06m (82ft 2.5in)
Max cruise speed: 480km/h (298mph)
Accommodation: 60 plus two crew
First aircraft flown: 24 November 1955
History: Designed by Fokker, with Netherlands government backing, the original P.275 was for a DC-3 replacement, with a shoulder wing, twin-Dart powered 32-seater. This subsequently evolved into the F27 of 1952. It was named Friendship on 23 March 1958. F27 Mk 200 (F27A) has improved powerplants; F27 Mk 300 (F27B) 'Combiplane' has a large forward cargo door; F27 Mk 400 (F27M) has improved powerplants; F27 Mk 500 has a 1.52m (5ft) longer fuselage and a large forward cargo door; F27 Mk 600 retains the shorter fuselage but has the other improvements of the Mk 500; FH227B to E have a 1.83m (6ft) longer fuselage of 25.5m (83ft 8in) and other improvements. Over 786 built when production ceased in 1986, including 206 in USA by Fairchild. Fokker production includes 85 Mk 100, 138 Mk 200, 13 Mk 300, 218 Mk 400/600, 112 Mk 500. Fairchild built 128 F27s and 78 FH227s. Most surviving corporate aircraft are Fairchild-Hiller F27s. These comprise: F27 — 2; F27F — 5; F27J — 4; FH227B — 2; FH227D — 1 and FH227E — 1.
Fokker-built corporate F27s: F27-100 — 1; F27-300 — 1; F227-500 — 6; F27-600 — 3.
Recognition: Twin turboprops set below high, straight wing. A slender oval section fuselage with pointed nose and tail; cabin windows are distinctively oval shaped. Tall fin and rudder with large dorsal extension. The small tailplane is set either side of base of rudder

Above:
Fokker F27. **PRM**

Below:
Fokker F27 Friendship. DJM

Above:
Grumman Gulfstream I. **APM**

Below:
Grumman G-159 Gulfstream I. **PRM**

Grumman G-159 Gulfstream I

Twin-turboprop business and corporate transport
Data for: Gulfstream I
Powerplant: Two 1648kW (2,210shp)
Rolls-Royce Dart 529-8X or -8E turboprops
Span: 23.92m (78ft 6in)
Length: 19.43m (63ft 9in)
Max cruise speed: 575km/h (357mph)
Accommodation: 10/14 passengers plus two crew
(could carry up to 19 passengers)
First aircraft flown: 14 August 1958

History: The Gulfstream I was produced as a civil executive transport based on the naval Grumman Tracker/Trader. It was the right design at the right time and demand was encouraging. With the advent of business jets the turboprop appeared an anachronism and Grumman embarked on the Gulfstream II jet. Delivered to large business corporations and heads of state worldwide. Some 25–30 of the 202 built were acquired for airline use, with up to 24 seats. A stretched Gulfstream IC Commuter, seating 38 passengers, flew on 25 October 1979, but did not enter production — and was offered for retrofit of existing Gulfstream Is. Typical executive layouts provided for 10 passengers plus a flight crew of two. Currently 107 are registered as corporate aircraft, mostly in North America.

Recognition: Low-wing, of equal taper and rounded tips. Noticeable dihedral. Circular fuselage, with five large oval windows on each side. Large engine nacelles, mainly above the wing. Swept fin with low-set dihedralled tailplane at rear fuselage extremity.

Above:
Gulfstream II-SP. *PRM*

Below:
Gulfstream II. *PRM*

Gulfstream Aerospace Gulfstream II

Twin-jet business and corporate transport
Data for: Gulfstream II
Powerplant: Two 50.77kN (11,400lb st) Rolls-
Royce Spey 511-8 turbofans
Span: 21.87m (71ft 9in) (over tip tanks)
Length: 24.36m (79ft 11in)
Max cruise speed: 936km/h (581mph)
Accommodation: 19 passengers plus two crew
First aircraft flown: 2 October 1966
History: The Gulfstream II was a low-wing aircraft
with twin jets hung on to the rear fuselage, and
the large oval windows that were so popular on
the turboprop Gulfstream I. 258 were built before

being replaced by the Gulfstream III in 1980. The long range of the Gulfstream II, evolved as a jet-powered derivative
of the Gulfstream I, put it in a class of its own when it was first introduced, and made it particularly attractive to the
larger companies with international operations. After the Gulfstream IIs had been built, the Rolls-Royce Spey
turbofans were retrofitted with acoustic 'hush kits' to meet more stringent environmental regulations. Typical
executive arrangement is 10 seats plus crew. Wing tip tanks were standard on aircraft delivered after 1975. The
aircraft could be converted to Gulfstream IIER standard with additional long-range tanks giving an extra 400 mile
range. Gulfstream IIB — a conversion of a Gulfstream II with a Gulfstream III wing. First flew on 17 March 1981.
Currently 236 Gulfstream IIs are registered to corporate users.
Recognition: Low-mounted swept wing. Slim circular fuselage with five oval windows on each side. Small pod-
mounted engines on each side of rear fuselage. Swept tail fin with swept T-tailplane.

Above:
Gulfstream Aerospace G-1159A Gulfstream III. **DJM**

Gulfstream Aerospace Gulfstream III
Twin-turbofan long-range business and corporate transport
Data for: Gulfstream III
Powerplant: Two 50.8kN (11,400lb st) Rolls-Royce Spey Mk 511-8 turbofans
Span: 23.7m (77ft 10in)
Length: 25.3m (83ft 1in)
Max cruise speed: 928km/h (577mph)
Accommodation: 19 passengers plus two/three crew
First aircraft flown: 2 December 1979
History: In 1976 Grumman American developed a brand-new Gulfstream III to replace the Gulfstream II. It had a 24in fuselage stretch, improved wing with leading edge extensions and winglets, new nose and cockpit. Military version known as C-20. Currently 166 Gulfstream IIIs are registered as corporate aircraft.
Recognition: Low-mounted swept wing with prominent winglets. Wings mounted in slight bulge, half-way along under fuselage. Slim oval fuselage with six oval windows on each side and front entry door on port side. Two pod-mounted engines, set high on each side of rear fuselage. Rear fuselage tapers to a point. Swept fin and rudder and swept T-tailplane.

Above:
Gulfstream Aerospace G-1159A Gulfstream III. **DJM**

Below:
Gulfstream Aerospace G-1159A Gulfstream III. **DJM**

Above:
Gulfstream Aerospace G-1159C Gulfstream IV.
Gulfstream Aerospace

Below:
Gulfstream Aerospace G-1159C Gulfstream IV. **PRM**

Gulfstream Aerospace Gulfstream IV

Twin-turbofan long-range business and corporate transport
Data for: Gulfstream IV
Powerplant: Two 61.6kN (13,850lb st)
Rolls-Royce Tay Mk 611-8 turbofans
Span: 23.72m (77ft 10in) (over winglets)
Length: 26.92m (88ft 4in)
Max cruise speed: 943km/h (586mph)
Accommodation: 14/19 passengers plus three crew
First aircraft flown: 19 September 1985

History: Introduced as a Gulfstream III with a 54in fuselage stretch, an extra cabin window on each side, a modified wing, glass cockpit and Tay turbofans. It is now being replaced by the Gulfstream IV-SP, with a wide body configuration and longer range. 1993 Gulfstream IV — an improved, higher weight version introduced in 1993. SRA-4 is the special missions version of the Gulfstream IV. C-20G is the passenger and cargo transport for the US Navy and features a large cargo door and convertible interior. Special missions versions are in service for electronic surveillance and reconnaissance, maritime patrol, ASW and medical evacuation. C-20 is a VIP version flown by the USAF. Currently 219 Gulfstream IVs are registered as corporate aircraft.

Recognition: Swept wing with pronounced winglets. Wings low-mounted in slight bulge, half-way along under fuselage. Slim oval fuselage with six oval windows on each side and front entry door on port side. Two pod-mounted engines, set high on each side of rear fuselage. Large cowlings. Rear fuselage tapers to a point. Swept fin and rudder and swept T-tailplane.

Above:
Hawker Siddeley HS748. **PRM**

Below:
Hawker Siddeley HS748. **DJM**

Hawker Siddeley HS748

Twin-turboprop short-range transport and corporate aircraft
Data for: HS748 Series 2B
Powerplant: Two 1,700kW (2,280shp) Rolls-Royce Dart 552 turboprops
Span: 31.23m (102ft 6in)   *Length:* 20.42m (67ft 0in)
Max cruise speed: 447km/h (277mph)
Accommodation: 52 plus two crew
First aircraft flown: 24 June 1960 (Series 1); June 1979 (Series 2)
History: Hawker Siddeley developed in the late 1950s a twin-turboprop transport for the short-haul market, basically a replacement for the DC-3 Dakota and Vickers Viking. It was in competition with the Fokker F27 that was already in test flight, and one of the design objectives set by Avro (eventually absorbed into Hawker Siddeley Aviation) was to offer an aircraft that was cheaper and had a better performance. The Series 1, 2 and 2A are all externally similar.
The Series 2B has a 1.22m (4ft) extension to the wing span and an optional freight door.
Production: 381, including 18 Series 1. In early 1996 11 HS748-2s were still in corporate use.
Recognition: Twin turboprops mounted above and forward of the low-set wing, with the undercarriage fairing beneath. Wings have dihedral and taper towards the tips. A broad, unswept fin and rudder with dorsal fillet. Low set tailplane either side of lower rear fuselage. Some versions have large, port side freight loading door at rear.

Above:
BAe 125 Srs 700B. **PRM**

Hawker Siddeley/BAe 125
Twin-engined business and corporate jet
Data for: HS125 Series 700
Powerplant: Two 16.48kN (3,700lb st) Garrett AiResearch TFE731-3-1H turbofans
Span: 14.33m (47ft 0in) *Length:* 15.46m (50ft 8.5in)
Max cruise speed: 808km/h (502mph) *Accommodation:* Eight/14 passengers plus two crew
First aircraft flown: 13 August 1962 (HS125 prototype); 21 January 1971 (Series 600); 28 June 1976 (Series 700)
History: Initially a business jet introduced by de Havilland and known as 'Jet Dragon'. It became part of the Hawker
Siddeley Group in January 1960 and became the HS125. Eight Series 1, with Viper engine, built; 77 Series 1A/B
built; 29 Series 3A/3B; Series 4 — marketed as the HS125-400A/400B — 116 built; Series 600 — 70;
Series 700 — 215. The first DH125s were Series I followed by the Series IA/IB. For longer range the 3A-R and
3B-R incorporated an extra fuel tank faired into the underside of the rear fuselage. A further series of refinements
marked the introduction of the Series 4, marketed as HS125-400A/400B. The Series 600 introduced a lengthened
fuselage with increased seating capacity. The Series 2 was a military version for the RAF known as Dominie. The
Series 700 introduced the turbofans in place of the Viper turbojets to achieve significant savings in fuel consumption
and therefore increased range. Both the Series 600 and Series 700 have a longer fuselage than earlier versions of
the type. BAe 125-731 — a series 400A retrofitted with TFE731-3 turbofans by Hawker Siddeley. BAe 125-F600B
— Series 600A retrofitted with TFE731-3 turbofans by Hawker Siddeley. BAe 700-II — factory refurbished
HS125-700. Currently 189 early 125s, 257 - 600 series and 296 - 800 series are registered to corporate users.
Recognition: Low swept wing, with square tips. Swept fin and rudder with extended dorsal fillet. Swept tailplane set
high on fin. Short deep ventral strake at rear fuselage extremity. Pod-mounted engines on each side of fuselage.
Six fuselage windows on each side with forward entry door.

Above:
BAe/HS125 Srs 400F. ***PRM***

Above:
Israel Aircraft Industries 1125 Astra SP. ***PRM***

Above:
Israel Aircraft Industries 1125 Astra SP. ***PRM***

Israel Aircraft Industries 1125 Astra
Twin-turbofan business and corporate transport
Data for: 1125 Astra
Powerplant: Two 16.23kN (3,650lb st) Garrett TFE731-3B-100G turbofans
Span: 16.05m (52ft 8in)
Length: 16.94m (55ft 7in)
Max cruise speed: 862km/h (535mph)
Accommodation: Six/nine passengers plus two crew
First aircraft flown: 19 March 1984
History: IAI developed an updated version of the Jet Commander — designated IAI-1123 Westwind I. The
Westwind II used a new 'Sigma' wing and has winglets. The current production model — the Astra, that only bears
a superficial resemblance to the original Jet Commander. The Astra features a swept wing using the 'Sigma'
technology. Production — Westwind I — 116; Westwind II — 90; Astra 704, production continues. Astra SP —
introduced 1989, with new interior and upgraded avionics known in the USA as Astra Jet. The Astra was developed
from the straight wing Westwind of which the first production example first flew on 5 October 1964. The Astra SPX
has TFE731-40R-200G turbofans, a revised interior and winglets. Currently 32 Astras and 38 Astra SPs are
registered as corporate aircraft.
Recognition: Swept wing (34° inboard, 25° outboard) — trailing edge sweep on outer panels. Mounted low
under fuselage midway. Oval fuselage, with upward taper at underneath rear. Raised cockpit. Five square windows
on each side and entry door at front, port side. Pod-mounted engines, mounted high on each side of rear fuselage.
Swept, slim fin, with rounded tip. Swept tailplane mounted low on fin.

Above:
BAe Jetstream 31. **PRM**

Below:
BAe Jetstream 3102. **DJM**

Jetstream Aircraft/BAe Jetstream Super 31

Twin-turboprop commuter airliner and corporate transport
Basic data for: Jetstream Super 31
Powerplant: Two 760kW (1,020shp) Allied Signal Garrett
TPE331-12UAR turboprops
Span: 15.87m (52ft 0in)
Length: 14.36m (47ft 1.5in)
Max cruise speed: 488km/h (303mph)
Accommodation: Eight/12 plus one/two crew
First aircraft flown: 28 March 1980; the original Handley
Page Jetstream was flown on 18 August 1967

History: The Jetstream was originally produced by Handley Page at Radlett, but the receivers were called in on 8 August 1969 — after 40 complete aircraft and 33 incomplete airframes had been produced. In 1972 all production rights were transferred to Scottish Aviation. The original Handley Page Jetstream has Turboméca Astazou XIV turboprops which are more slender and extend further forward of the wing, with a distinctive long spinner. The Super 31 developed by British Aerospace has uprated engines — Garrett TPE331-12 turboprops, improved cabin and increased max take-off weight. The -41 is a 29-seat stretched version (19.25m/63ft 2in) with two 1,118kW (1,500shp) Allied Signal Garrett TPE331-14GR/HR and glass cockpit. Production: 390 Jetstream 31/Super 31 delivered by late-1995, the USA's regional airline industry being the biggest market. Jetstream Aircraft offers corporate versions of the Jetstream 31 Corporate Shuttle and Jetstream 41 Corporate Shuttle with eight and 12 seats respectively. A number of J31s have been converted from airliner to corporate use by Stevens Aviation in the USA and offered through Jetstream's dealer network.

Recognition: Twin turboprops mounted above and forward of the low-set wings. Circular fuselage with long, pointed nose forward of cockpit. Swept, tall fin and rudder with a triangular ventral extension. Circular cabin windows and passenger door aft of port wing for the 31, forward for the 41.

Above:
Learjet 24. **PRM**

Below:
Learjet 24. **PRM**

Learjet 23/24/25

Medium-range business and corporate jet
Data for: Gates Learjet 25D
Powerplant: Two 13.14kN (2,950lb st)
General Electric CJ6106 turbojets
Span: 10.84m (35ft 7in) (over tip tanks)
Length: 14.50m (47ft 7in)
Max cruise speed: 859km/h (534mph)
Accommodation: Six passengers plus two crew
First aircraft flown: 7 October 1963 (Learjet 23);
12 August 1966 (Learjet 25)
History: Founded in 1960 by William P. Lear to
manufacture a high-speed twin-jet executive aircraft
known as the Learjet 23. It has been steadily developed and built in large numbers. The Learjet 25 is 1.27m (4ft
2in) longer than the 23/24. The 23 was the original model. The 24A had slightly larger engines. 24C an economy
model with no fuselage tank and 24D increased range version. There are currently 262 Learjet 23/24s and 336
Learjet 25s on the civil register as corporate aircraft.
Recognition: Low wing with swept leading edge and straight trailing edge and wing tip tanks. Streamlined circular
fuselage. Slightly swept tail fin and swept T-tailplane. Small dorsal fillet to fin and ventral strake at rear. Number and
size of windows vary with model. Twin pod-mounted engines at rear on either side of fuselage. Front port entry door.
Early versions had tailplane/fin bullet.

Above:
Learjet 55C. **PRM**

Below:
Learjet 55. **DJM**

Learjet 28/29/55/60
Medium-range business and corporate jet
Data for: Learjet 55C
Powerplant: Two 16.47kN (3,700lb st)
Garrett AirResearch TFE731-3A turbofans
Span: 13.35m (43ft 9.5in)
Length: 16.79m (55ft 1in)
Max cruise speed: 843km/h (524mph)
Accommodation: Two flight deck crew plus
four/eight passengers

First aircraft flown: 21 August 1978 (Learjet 28); 19 April 1979 (Learjet 55); 13 June 1991 (Learjet 60).
History: The Learjet 28 is an improved version of the Learjet 25 and has a redesigned supercritical wing with
vertical winglets at the tips. The Learjet 29 Longhorn is the long-range version but is externally very similar. Learjet
married a new wide-body 10-passenger fuselage to the wing of the 28/29 to produce the Learjet 55. In June
1990, it was acquired by the Canadian company, Bombardier Inc, and the name changed to Learjet Inc. The 55C
and 55C/ER are the extended-range versions and the 55CLR, the long-range version. The 60 is a 10-passenger
development of the 55 with a 43in fuselage stretch and two 20.49kN (4,600lb st) Pratt & Whitney PW305
turbofans and replaced the Model 55 in 1992. There are currently five Learjet 28s, four Learjet 29s, 140 Learjet
55s and 78 Learjet 60s registered with corporate owners.
Recognition: Low wing with swept leading edge and straight trailing edge. Vertical winglets at the tips. Long, slim
circular fuselage. Slightly swept fin and rudder and swept T-tailplane. Small dorsal fillet to fin and ventral strake at
rear. Pod-mounted engines high on rear fuselage. Five small square cabin windows on each side. Front port entry
door. The final version, 55C introduced in 1988, has two 'delta fins' mounted on the lower rear fuselage.

Above:
Learjet 31. ***Learjet***

Learjet 31A, 35A and 36A

Light twin-turbofan business and corporate jet
Data for: Learjet 35A/36A
Powerplant: Two 15.6kN (3,500lb st) Garrett TFE731-2-2B turbofans
Span: 12.04m (39ft 6in) (over tip tanks)
Length: 14.83m (48ft 8in)
Max cruise speed: 852km/h (529mph)
Accommodation: Eight passengers plus two crew
First aircraft flown: 4 January 1973 (Model 26); 11 May 1987 (Model 31A); 13 June 1991 (Model 60)
History: Originally known as the Gates Learjet, the name of the company was later changed to Lear Jet Industries. Production: Learjet 31 — 34; 31A — 70 plus and still in production; Learjet 35 — 66; 35A — 620 plus, still in production; Learjet 60 — 45 plus, still in production. Model 31 has Model 55 wings incorporating winglets — but no tip tanks. Model 35 is a Model 25 with a 13in fuselage stretch. Model 60 is a 10-passenger development of the Model 55 with 43in fuselage stretch. Current production models are 35A and six-seat, longer range 36A. A variety of military/paramilitary versions have been produced — 80 are in service with the USAF, designated C-21A. PC-35A is the maritime patrol version, RC-35A — reconnaissance, VC-35A - utility version, U-36A — version for Japanese Maritime Self-Defence Force. The 31A has the fuselage and powerplant of the 35A/36A with the wing of Learjet 55. Currently there are 126 Learjet 31s, 33 Learjet 35s and 36 Learjet 36s registered to corporate users.
Recognition: Slightly swept wings, with straight trailing edge. Wing tip tanks with small fins at rear. Wings low-mounted half-way along fuselage. Narrow circular fuselage with pointed nose. Tapered rear fuselage with ventral strake at extreme rear. Swept large fin and rudder, with swept T-tail. Engines pod-mounted on sides of rear fuselage. Four windows on each side of fuselage. Front entry door on port side. 31A has delta fins added and is fitted with winglets — no tip tanks. Five windows on each side.

Above:
LET L-410UVP-E16A Turbolet. **DJM**

Below:
LET L-410AB Turbolet. **PRM**

LET L-410 Turbolet

Twin-turboprop light and corporate transport
Data for: LET L-410UVP-E20
Powerplant: Two 560kW (750shp)
Motorlet Walter M601-E turboprops
Span: 19.98m (65ft 6in)
Length: 14.42m (47ft 4in)
Max cruise speed: 380km/hr (236mph)
Accommodation: 17/19 plus two crew
First aircraft flown: 16 April 1969;
L-410UVP-E first flown 30 December 1984
History: Design of the LET L-410 was started in
1966 and was for a twin-turboprop light transport intended primarily for use on local transport and freight services with the ability to operate from airfields with a natural grass surface. Originally produced for Aeroflot and other airlines, mainly in Eastern Europe. Early production L-410A had Pratt & Whitney PT6A turboprops; the L-410M introduced Motorlet M601 powerplants. The L-410UVP with a slightly larger fuselage, extended wing tips, taller fin and rudder and other detailed changes was produced until 1985. The L-410UVP-E20 accommodates four more passengers, has new engines driving five-blade propellers and wing tip fuel tanks. The UVP-E20 Model 420 first flew on 11 November 1993 and has more powerful 580kW M601 F engines and other improvements. Over 1,000 L-410s had been delivered by late 1995 and a number are in use as corporate aircraft.
Recognition: Engines mounted below and forward of the high-set straight leading edge wing with wing tip tanks. A short, oval section fuselage with a long tapered nose forward of the cockpit. Seven rectangular cabin windows, with large cabin door just aft of wing. Large undercarriage fairings extend out from lower fuselage. A slightly swept, tall, angular fin and rudder with ventral extension below tail cone. Straight, dihedralled tailplane is mounted on fin above fuselage.

Above:
Lockheed JetStar II. **via M. J. Hooks**

Below:
Lockheed L1329 JetStar. **Ian MacFarlane**

Lockheed JetStar

Four-turbofan executive and corporate transport
Data for: JetStar II
Powerplant: Four 16.48kN (3,700lb st)
Garrett AiResearch TFE731-3 turbofans
Span: 16.60m (54ft 5in)
Length: 18.42m (60ft 5in)
Max cruise speed: 817km/h (507.7mph)
Accommodation: Up to 10 passengers plus two
crew

First aircraft flown: 4 September 1957 (JetStar I); 10 July 1974 (JetStar 731); 18 August 1976 (JetStar II)
History: Lockheed developed the JetStar I as a private venture, to meet USAF requirements for a utility jet transport, initially powered by two Bristol Siddeley Orpheus turbojets. Production models had four 14.70kW (3,300lb st) JT12A-8 turbojets. Production of 162 JetStars ended in 1973. In 1974 Garrett AiResearch developed the JetStar 731 conversion with TFE731 turbofans, and Lockheed subsequently built 40 of the similar JetStar II version. The last JetStar was delivered on 23 April 1980. Currently 116 are registered as corporate aircraft. Sixteen C-140B were delivered to the USAF as a VIP transport and for navaid calibration. The initial civil JetStar was the L-1329-23A JetStar Dash-6, with later models designated Dash-8. A number of JetStars have been converted to turbofan power by AiResearch and are known as JetStar 731s.
Recognition: Low swept wing mounted half-way along lower fuselage. Four engines are pod-mounted, two on either side of rear fuselage. Swept leading edge to fin and rudder, with small air intake at base of fin. Long-range tanks (shortened on the II) are pod-mounted midway along leading edge of wing. Swept tailplane set midway on fin. Five square cabin windows on each side of fuselage.

Above:
Mitsubishi MU-2 Marquise. **PRM**
Right:
Mitsubishi MU-2M. **PRM**

Mitsubishi MU-2 Marquise/Solitaire

Twin-turboprop utility/business and corporate transport
Data for: Marquise
Powerplant: Two 580.2kW (778shp)
AiResearch TPE331-10-501M turboprops
Span: 11.95m (39ft 2in)   *Length:* 12.02m (39ft 5in)
Max cruise speed: 574km/h (357mph)   *Accommodation:* Six or seven passengers plus two crew
First aircraft flown: 14 September 1963 (MU-2A Astazou); 11 March 1965 (MU-2B TPE331); 10 January 1969 (MU-2G)
History: In 1959 Mitsubishi decided to return to aircraft manufacture and was one of the first manufacturers to see the possibilities of turboprop engines. The high-speed performance is aided by a unique wing design which abandons conventional ailerons in favour of a system of retractable spoilers. Production ceased in 1986 after 831 MU-2s had been built (including 73 military versions). MU-2B has the AiResearch engines; MU-2D (18 built) had integral tanks and higher weights; MU-2F (95 built) had uprated engines and larger wing tip tanks; MU-2F had 1.90m (6ft 2.75in) fuselage stretch and external fairings on fuselage sides to house the main undercarriage; MU-2J - long fuselage with uprated engines; MU-2K - an 'F' with uprated engines; MU-2L and MU-2M — increased gross weights; MU-2N and MU-2P had larger diameter, slow-running propellers to reduce cabin noise. Final versions were the Marquise and Solitaire with uprated engines and larger fuel tanks. MU-2E is used by the Japanese Air Self-Defence Force for rescue work. The type is popular in the US because of its ability to operate from short rough airfields — a rare characteristic in business aircraft. Currently there are 386 MU-2s (of all versions) registered as corporate aircraft.
Recognition: High-mounted wing, with straight leading edge. Large wing tip tanks. Very small engine nacelles. Circular stubby fuselage. Two windows on each side of short version and four windows on lengthened version. Twin ventral strakes under rear fuselage. Swept fin with pronounced forward fillet. Low mounted tailplane, with distinctive small fillet at base of leading edge. Lengthened version has bulged ventral section to house main wheels.

Above:
Mooney M20R Ovation. ***M. J. Hooks***

Mooney M20-201/231

Single-engined four-seat light and corporate aircraft

Basic data for: Mooney M20R Ovation

Powerplant: One 224kW (300hp) Teledyne Continental I O-550G flat-six non-turbocharged piston engine

Span: 11.0m (36ft 1in)

Length: 7.52m (24ft 8in)

Max cruise speed: 338km/h (210mph) ***Accommodation:*** Pilot plus three passengers

First aircraft flown: 10 August 1953 (M20); June 1976 (201); October 1976 (231)

History: The original Mooney company built more than 5,400 series of four-seaters (M-20C Mark 21 Ranger, M-20E Super-21 Chaparral and M-20F Executive) up to 1972, when financial difficulties prevailed. Production resumed in 1974. M20 — initial metal/wood version with 111.8kW (150hp) O-320 engine; M20B/C-Mark 21 — all metal, new windscreen; M20E-Super 21 — With 149.1kW (200hp) Lycoming engine and refinements. Also named Aerostar 201 and Chaparral following purchase of Mooney by Butler Aviation; M20F Executive/Aerostar 201 — Stretched (10in) cabin, three side windows and 149.1kW (200hp) Lycoming IO-360-A3B6D; M20J/Mooney 201/205 — Modified nose, windscreen and two longer cabin windows; M20K/Mooney 231/252 — 201 with 156.6kW (210hp) turbocharged Continental engine; Mooney TLS — formerly M20M introduced 1989 with 201.3kW (270hp) turbocharged Textron Lycoming TIO-540-AF1A. The Mooney features the distinctive fin and rudder with its unswept leading edge. The M20R Ovation is produced as a corporate aircraft and is claimed to be the world's highest performing normally aspirated production aircraft. Mooney production: M20 — 200; M20A — 500; M20B — 225; M20C — 2131; M20D — 160; M20E — 1,475; M20F — 1251; M20G — 196; M22 — 39; M20J-R — 3,245+. A considerable number are used as a corporate aircraft.

Recognition: Single-engined low-wing all-metal monoplane with retractable tricycle undercarriage. Recognisable by vertical leading edge to fin and rudder and swept forward trailing edge. Straight leading edge to wings and tailplane. Pronounced fillet at front wing roots.

Above:
North American/Rockwell Sabreliner. **PRM**

Below:
North American/Rockwell Sabreliner. **PRM**

North American/Rockwell Sabreliner

Twin-jet business and corporate transport
Data for: Sabreliner Srs 65
Powerplant: Two 16.48kN (3,700lb st)
Garrett AiResearch TFE731-3-1D turbofans
Span: 15.37m (50ft 5.25in)
Length: 14.30m (46ft 11in)
Max cruise speed: 850km/h (530mph)
Accommodation: Ten passengers plus two crew

First aircraft flown: 1958 (T-39A); 15 December 1976 (Sabreliner 60); 29 June 1977 (Sabreliner 65);
8 September 1978 (Sabreliner 60A)

History: A version similar to the military trainer was offered for commercial use as a business transport (Sabreliner 40) and over 125 had been built when production ceased in the early 1970s. A total of 159 military examples were built including the T-39A, T-39B and T-39D. Sabreliner 60 was the original version. The 65 featured an advanced wing design and Garrett engines. Those with the designation A have been retrofitted with the new wing. The Sabreliner 80A is the 75A with the Raisbeck new wing. It was originally supplied to the USAF and US Navy as the T-39 and CT-39, and was developed into the Series 40 and 60 executive transports. Military versions had the Pratt & Whitney JT12A turbojets. The Sabreliner 40R is a factory modified Model 40 with a Model 60 interior. Sabreliner 60/TF — a factory modified Model 60 with Garrett TFE731 turbofans. Sabreliner 75 — a Model 60 with raised cabin roof. Currently there are 16 Sabreliner T-39s; 86 Sabreliner 40s; one Sabreliner 50; 114 Sabreliner 60s; six Sabreliner 75s; 56 Sabreliner 75A80A series and 77 Sabreliner 65s registered as corporate aircraft.

Recognition: Low swept wing mounted half-way along short, stocky fuselage. Prominent raised cockpit canopy. Pod-mounted engines on either side of rear fuselage, with intakes level with trailing edge of wing. Swept tailplane mounted on rear fuselage extremity. Slightly swept fin and rudder with small dorsal fillet. Five unusual triangular cabin windows on each side of fuselage, with front entry door.

Above:
Partenavia P68B. **PRM**

Below:
Partenavia P68B. **PRM**

Partenavia P68 Victor

Twin-engined six/seven-seat light and corporate aircraft
Data for: Partenavia P68C
Powerplant: Two 149kW (200hp)
Lycoming IO-360-A1B6 piston engines
Span: 12.0m (39ft 4in) *Length:* 9.55m (31ft 4in)
Max cruise speed: 307km/h (191mph)
Accommodation: Pilot plus up to six passengers
First aircraft flown: 25 May 1970 (P68); 11 September
1978 (P68T); 20 November 1981 (A68TP-30)

History: In 1970 Partenavia introduced its most successful design — the P68, to supplement its well-established Oscar family of single-engined two/four-seaters. It was aimed at a range of business and utility users. It has been flown on floats and is produced with turbocharged engines. P68 — original version; P68B — P68 with 6in fuselage stretch, standard six-seat interior; P68 Observer — P68B with fully glazed nose section designed for police and observation duties developed by Sportavia-Pützer in Germany; P68C — P68B with longer nose; P68C-TC — with 156.6kW (210hp) Lycoming TIO-360-C1A6D turbocharged engines; AP68TP-300 Spartacus — a P68T with fixed undercarriage, redesigned tailplane and upturned wing tips; AP68TP-600 Viator, developed jointly with Aeritalia — Spartacus with retractable undercarriage, lengthened nose, stretched fuselage and Allison 250-B17C engines. Production: P68 Series — 392+; AP68 TP-300/600 - 20+, with 12 of the latter in use as corporate aircraft. Partenavia was purchased by AerCosmos of Milan in 1993. Taneja Aerospace and Aviation of India is undertaking licence production of the P68 range in Bangalore and the first aircraft were delivered in 1995.

Recognition: High-wing monoplane with underslung engines. Sleek fuselage and streamlined nose. Swept fin and rudder with small dorsal fillet. Low set oblong tailplane with fillet at forward base. Three large cabin windows on each side. Fixed tricycle undercarriage with spats.

Above:
Piaggio P.180 Avanti. **PRM**

Below:
Piaggio P.180 Avanti. **PRM**

Piaggio P.180 Avanti

Twin-turboprop high-speed corporate transport
Data for: P.180 Avanti
Powerplant: Two 1,107kW (1,485shp) Pratt & Whitney Canada PT6A-66 turboprops
Span: 14.03m (46ft 0.5in)
Length: 14.41m (47ft 3.5in)
Max cruise speed: 482km/h (299mph)
Accommodation: Nine passengers plus one/two crew
First aircraft flown: 23 September 1986
History: In October 1983 Gates Learjet and Piaggio joined forces to design the GP-180 Avanti twin-turboprop business aircraft which would compete with the Beech Starship. In 1986 Learjet pulled out of the partnership but Piaggio continued with the project. Following a severe financial crisis in 1994, Piaggio entered into a sales and development partnership with Grumman to market the Avanti. Currently there are 21 P.180s registered as corporate aircraft.

Recognition: Three-surface control with canard foreplane and T-tail to allow unobstructed cabin with maximum headroom to be placed forward of mid-mounted wing along fuselage. Straight leading edge to shoulder-mounted wing. Pusher turboprops aft of cabin. Cigar shaped fuselage. Swept fin/rudder and swept tailplane. Twin ventral strakes at rear. Six windows on port side of fuselage plus door - seven on starboard side. Tailplane has slight anhedral.

Above:
Pilatus Britten-Norman BN-2A Islander. *PRM*

Pilatus Britten-Norman Islander/Turbine Islander

Twin-piston/turboprop light and corporate transport
Data for: BN-2T Turbine Islander
Powerplant: Two 298kW (400shp) Allison 250-B17C turboprops
Span: 14.94m (49ft 0in); [16.15m (53ft) with extended wing tip tanks]
Length: 10.86m (35ft 7.75in)   *Max cruise speed:* 315km/h (196mph)
Accommodation: Nine plus one crew
First aircraft flown: 13 June 1965 (BN-2 Continental IO-360);
Turbine Islander 2 August 1980 (BN-2T Allison 250)
History: The Islander was designed in the early 1960s as an all-metal twin-engined utility aircraft that had the minimum of refinements and was fitted with a fixed undercarriage and simple systems to allow maintenance away from normal aircraft workshops. The BN-2, BN-2A and BN-2B are all broadly similar piston-engined versions. The BN-2B-20 has two 225kW Textron Lycoming O-540 piston engines and the BN-2B-26 two 195kW O-540s. The latter two variants could have optional extras which include a lengthened nose forward of the cockpit and/or 1.22m (4ft) extended wing tips. The BN-2T has smaller Allison 250 turboprops in place of the Lycoming series piston engines. Over 1,200 delivered by late 1995. Production lines are now located in Romania (IAV Bucuresti) and the Philippines (PADC). Production is approximately 20 per year. Pilatus Britten-Norman now offers the turboprop - and piston-powered BN-2 Islander in corporate form.
Recognition: Engines mounted below and forward of straight, high-set 'plank' wing. Fixed tricycle undercarriage with main wheels on extended, faired leg at rear of engines and nosewheel situated well forward below nose cone. Slab-sided rectangular fuselage with level top surface and gently raked lower surface aft of wing, two port-side cabin entry doors and large rectangular cabin windows. The tall, angular fin and rudder has small dorsal fillet; straight tailplane mounted on top of fuselage, below rudder. The extended wing tips on some aircraft have distinctive conical camber.

Above:
Pilatus PC-6 Turbo-Porter.
PRM

Right:
Pilatus PC-6/B2-H4
Turbo-Porter. **PRM**

Pilatus PC-6 Turbo-Porter

Single-turboprop light STOL and corporate transport
Data for: PC-6/B2-H2 Turbo-Porter
Powerplant: One 410kW (550shp) Pratt & Whitney
Canada PT6A — 27 turboprop
Span: 15.13m (49ft 8in)
Length: 11.00m (36ft 1in)   *Max cruise speed:* 259km/h (161mph)
Accommodation: Up to nine passengers (high density layout) plus pilot
First aircraft flown: 4 May 1959 (piston); 2 May 1961 (turboprop)
History: In 1959 Pilatus marketed the general purpose utility STOL Porter, developed from the P-4. Initially powered by a Lycoming piston engine, it subsequently received turboprop power with a Turboméca Astazou engine. Pilatus produced the PC-6/B version with the Canadian engine to make the aircraft more saleable in the USA. This has been the standard powerplant since 1966. At least a third of production Turbo-Porters have been delivered to military users. The US Air Force purchased the PC-6C as the AU-23A for close support forward combat duties. The PC-6/AX-H2 has the Turboméca Astazou X turboprop and the PC-6/A1-H2 the Astazou XIIE turboprop. The PC-6/C1-H2 is the Fairchild version with the 428.8kW (575shp) Garrett TPE331-1-100 turboprop. The PC-6/B2-H4 has an enlarged dorsal fin and extended wing tips. Production of the PC-6/B2-H4 Turbo-Porter continues in Switzerland and some 405 examples have been built, plus approximately 90 built by Fairchild as Garrett-engined 'Heli-Porters' in the USA. Some 68 are registered as corporate aircraft.

Recognition: Square-sided fuselage with very long nose forward of cabin, tapering to small turboprop engine. High square-tipped wings, rectangular fin and rudder. Fixed undercarriage with large wheels and tyres, braced to the fuselage sides. Small tailwheel at rear fuselage extremity.

Above:
Pilatus PC-12. Peter J. Cooper

Below:
Pilatus PC-12. **PRM**

Pilatus PC-12

Single-turboprop pressurised utility/business and corporate
transport
Data for: PC-12P
Powerplant: One 880kW (1,180shp) Pratt & Whitney
Canada PT6A-67B turboprop
Span: 16.23m (53ft 3in)
Length: 14.38m (47ft 2.25in)
Max cruise speed: 435km/h (270mph)
Accommodation: Nine passengers plus one/two crew
First aircraft flown: 31 May 1991

History: The current major Pilatus project is the PC-12 - named 'PC-XII' when launched in 1989. It is a single-engined
multi-purpose utility aircraft aimed at the same market that has been successfully developed by the Cessna Caravan I.
PC-12P — nine-passenger version with six seats in a business layout; PC-12F — freighter version; Combi — four
passengers, plus freight capacity; Military — transport, parachute training, ambulance and other missions — high
density seating for 14. PC-12 Executive — a six-passenger layout. Currently there are 29 corporate registered PC-12s.
Recognition: Straight leading edge to low-mounted wing. Wedge shaped winglets. Oval fuselage, tapering at rear.
Sharply raked windscreen. Swept fin incorporating dorsal fillet with T-tailplane. Main gear retracts into wings. Tail fin
extends under rear fuselage. Four oval windows on each side of fuselage. Entry door at front on port side. Prominent
engine exhaust each side.

Above:
Piper PA-23-250 Aztec E. **DJM**

Below:
Piper PA-23-250 Aztec E. **PRM**

Piper PA-23 Apache/Aztec

Twin-engined four/six-seat light business and corporate aircraft

Data for: Piper PA-23-250 Aztec E
Powerplant: Two 186kW (250hp)
Lycoming IO-540-C4B5 piston engines
Span: 11.37m (37ft.4in)
Length: 9.52m (31ft 3in)
Max cruise speed: 332km/h (206mph)
Accommodation: Pilot plus three/five passengers
First aircraft flown: 2 March 1952 (Apache); 1959 (Aztec A)

History: The first Piper twin was originally known as the Twin-Stinson and became the PA-23-160 Apache, being Piper's first major entry in the twin-engined market. The 1959 Aztec A evolved into the six-seat longer-nosed Aztec B in 1962 followed by the Aztec C introduced in 1970. PA-23 Apache — light twin developed from the Twin-Stinson; PA-23-250 Aztec B — with longer nose incorporating baggage compartment, six-seat interior; PA-23-250 Aztec C/D/E/F — improved versions with optional turbocharged engines. Production: Apache — 2,165; Aztec — 4,812. Though now out of production for many years, there are a considerable number in corporate use.

Recognition: Twin-engined low-wing monoplane. Retractable tricycle undercarriage. Wings of equal chord with rounded tips. Pronounced fillet at front wing roots. Three glazed windows on each side. Apache has short nose, curved fin, rudder and tailplane. Aztec has more bulbous cabin, larger square-cut slightly swept fin and rudder and square-cut tailplane. The revised designations denoted updated equipment and fittings rather than any change in outline.

Above:
Piper PA-30-160 Twin Comanche B. **PRM**

Below:
Piper PA-30-160 Twin Comanche. **DJM**

Piper PA-30/39 Twin Comanche

Twin-engined four/six-seater business aircraft
Data for: Piper PA-39 Twin Comanche C/R
Powerplant: Two 119kW (160hp) Lycoming
IO-320-B1A piston engines
Span: 11.22m (36ft 9in)
Length: 7.67m (25ft 2in)
Max cruise speed: 319km/h (198mph)
Accommodation: Pilot plus three/five passengers
First aircraft flown: 7 November 1962

History: Piper developed the PA-30 as a twin version of the PA-24 Comanche single-engined light aircraft. Many variants were produced, these differing mainly in engine output, propellers and interior layout. PA-30 Twin Comanche B — third cabin window on each side and optional fifth/sixth seats, optional turbocharged engine; PA-30 Twin Comanche C — improved IO-320 engines, optional wing tip tanks; PA 39 Twin Comanche C/R — with contra-rotating propellers to eliminate torque effects. Also Rajay turbocharged option with TIO-320-C1A engines. Production: PA-30 — 2,001; PA-39 — 155. Though out of production for some time, a considerable number of PA-39s are used as corporate aircraft.

Recognition: Low-wing twin-engined monoplane with retractable tricycle undercarriage. Straight leading wing edge with pronounced fillet at front wing root. Engines mounted high on leading edge of wing. Swept fin and rudder with low-set tapered tailplane. Some models have wing tip fuel tanks.

Above:
Piper PA-31 Turbo Navajo. **PRM**

Below:
Piper PA-31-310 Turbo Navajo C. **PRM**

Piper PA-31 Navajo/Chieftain

Twin-piston/turbocharged commuter airliner, executive
and corporate aircraft
Data for: PA-31 Navajo
Powerplant: Two 242.5kW (325hp)
Lycoming TIO-540 piston engines
Span: 12.40m (40ft 8in)
Length: 9.94m (32ft 7.5in)
Max cruise speed: 409km/h (254mph)

Accommodation: Four/six passengers plus two crew
First aircraft flown: 30 September 1964 (PA-31); March 1968 (PA-31P)
History: Some 2,500 examples of the Navajo series were built and are in service with air taxi and commuter airlines
worldwide and particularly in the USA. Currently 696 are used as corporate aircraft. The Navajo B has turbocharged
TIO-540-E engines and optional pilot entry door. Chieftain has a 2ft fuselage stretch with 10-seat interior, one extra
window each side and cargo door. Powered by two countra-rotating Lycoming TIO-540-J2BD engines. PA-31P-425
is the pressurised Navajo with one window less on the port side, smaller windshield and two 313kW (425hp) TIGO-
541-E1A6 engines. Chieftain II has 4ft longer span wings and a PA-31T tailplane and 260kW (350hp) TIO-540-X48
countra-rotating engines.
Recognition: Low wing, with straight leading edge. 45° fillet between fuselage and engine nacelles. Long nacelles
protruding forward of wings. Square tips. Slim pointed nose, generous glazed areas. Port entry door at rear.
Swept fin and rudder with small dorsal fillet. Angular tailplane set at extremity of pointed rear fuselage.

Above:
Piper PA-31T Cheyenne II. **PRM**

Below:
Piper PA-31T Cheyenne II-XL. **PRM**

Piper PA-31T Cheyenne II

Six/eight-passenger corporate and business aircraft
Data for: Cheyenne II
Powerplant: Two 462kW (620shp)
Pratt & Whitney Canada PT6A-28 turboprops
Span: 14.53m (47ft 8in)
Length: 11.16m (38ft 0in)
Max cruise speed: 558km/h (346mph)
Accommodation: Six/eight including two crew
First aircraft flown: 20 August 1969

History: The Cheyenne is basically a turboprop-powered version of the pressurised Navajo — as indicated by the common PA-31 type number. It was added to the Piper range in 1974 as the company's first turbine-engined business aircraft. It features tip tanks to obtain extra fuel capacity, thus offering a greater range. In late 1977 Piper introduced a low-cost version, as the Cheyenne I with lower rated 373kW (500shp) Pratt & Whitney PT6A-11 engines. Use of tip tanks was optional. 202 Cheyenne Is, 17 IAs, 218 IIs and 81 II-XLs were registered to corporate users in early 1996.

Recognition: Low wing, with straight leading edge. 45° fillet between fuselage and engine nacelles. Long nacelles protruding forward of wings. Wing tip tanks usually fitted. Long, slim pointed nose. Three cabin windows on each side of the I and four on the II-XL. Swept tail fin with small dorsal fillet. Angular tailplane set at extremity of pointed rear fuselage.

Above:
Piper PA-32-300 Cherokee Six E. *PRM*

Below:
Piper PA-32RT-300 Lance II. *PRM*

Piper PA-32 Cherokee Six/Lance

Single-engined light business aircraft
Data for: A-32RT-300 Lance II
Powerplant: One 223.7kW (300hp) Lycoming TIO-540-S1AD turbocharged piston engine
Span: 10.0m (32ft 10in)
Length: 8.44m (27ft 8.5in)
Max cruise speed: 264km/h (164mph)
Accommodation: Five plus one crew
First aircraft flown: 6 December 1963 (Cherokee Six);
30 August 1974 (Lance)

History: The original Cherokee Six was basically a PA-28-235 with an 0.76m (2ft 6in) fuselage stretch with six seats (plus optional seventh seat) and powered by a 186.4kW (250hp) Lycoming O-540 engine. There are three main versions of the Lance — the original model was essentially a retractable-undercarriage Cherokee Six and featured a conventional tail unit. The Lance II and Turbo Lance II both have the T-tail configuration and the Turbo Lance has the extra power of a turbocharged engine. Over 4,400 Cherokee Six and 2,808 Cherokee Lance were produced and many are registered to corporate/business users.

Recognition: Large single-engined low-wing monoplane with retractable tricycle undercarriage. Equal chord wing with rounded tips. Four windows on each side. Most models have T-tail. Large air inlet beneath propeller spinner.

Above:
Piper PA-32R-301 Saratoga SP. ***PRM***

Below:
Piper PA-32R-301 Saratoga SP. ***DJM***

Piper PA-32 Saratoga

Single-engined liaison, training, communications and corporate aircraft

Data for: Saratoga IIHP

Powerplant: One 223.7kW (300hp) Lycoming IO-540-K1G5 piston engine

Span: 11.02m (36ft 2in)

Length: 8.44m (27ft 8in)

Max cruise speed: 282km/h (175mph)

Accommodation: Five/six plus one crew

First aircraft flown: 6 December 1963 (Cherokee Six)

History: The stretched PA Cherokee Six airframes grew into the retractable gear Saratoga SP. It was produced in four versions — a basic model with fixed or retractable undercarriage and two corresponding turbocharged models. PA-32P-301 Saratoga SP was without the T-tail, fitted with a Lance II retractable undercarriage. Saratoga IIHP, with the 300hp Lycoming engine, new cowling with round intakes, reduced-depth side windows and revised instrument panel. PA-32-301 Saratoga — had a new semi-tapered wing based on that of the PA-28-151 Warrior. PA-32-301T Turbo Saratoga — with turbocharged 300hp Lycoming TIO-540-S1AD engine in new cowling. PA-32R-301T Turbo Saratoga — PA-332-301T (without T-tail) and fitted with Lance II retractable undercarriage. Production: PA-32 Cherokee Six/Saratoga — 4,432. A considerable number are registered with business users.

Recognition: Resembles the Cherokee Six, in having four windows per side, but has longer span wings. Semi-tapered wings. Long tapering fuselage, swept tail fin with small dorsal fillet. Oblong tailplane mounted at rear fuselage extremity. Usually fixed undercarriage with large wheel spats. Four cabin windows, of varying size and shape, on each side of fuselage. Entry door at port rear.

Above:
Piper PA-34-200T Seneca II. **PRM**

Below:
Piper PA-34 Seneca III. **PRM**

Piper PA-34 Seneca

Twin-engined six-passenger light and corporate transport and trainer

Data for: Piper PA-34T Seneca II
Powerplant: Two 149kW (200hp) Continental TSIO-360-E flat-four turbocharged piston engines
Span: 11.85m (38ft 11in)
Length: 8.73m (28ft 7in)
Max cruise speed: 285km/h (219mph)
Accommodation: Pilot plus five passengers
First aircraft flown: 30 August 1968

History: The Seneca, among the lightest of the six-seat business twins on the market, was derived from the single-engined PA-32 Cherokee Six, of which it is in effect a twin-engined version. Licence production of the Seneca II began in Poland in 1979 as the PZL-M20 Mewa. In Brazil, Embraer builds the Seneca II as the EMB-810C. The PA-34 is basically a PA-32 with nose removed and two engines installed, retractable undercarriage, increased wing span and larger tail. PA-34-200 Seneca — original model with two 134.2kW (180hp) Lycoming O-360 piston engines; PA-34-200T Seneca II — turbocharged Seneca, optional club seating, seventh seat; PA-34-220T Seneca III — with two turbocharged 164kW (220hp), Continental TSIO-360-KB2A engines and single-piece windscreen; PA-34-220T Seneca IV has reduced-depth side windows, new engine cowlings with round air intakes, upgraded interior trim and new instrument panel. Total production of the Seneca was 4,562. A considerable number are in use as corporate aircraft.

Recognition: Twin-engined low-wing monoplane. Engines set high on leading edge of wings. Long pointed nose. Tapering fuselage. Four cabin windows each side. Wings of parallel chord with rounded tips. Pronounced fillet at front wing root. Swept fin and rudder. Low-mounted oblong tailplane.

Above:
Piper PA-42-720 Cheyenne IIIA. **PRM**

Below:
Piper PA-42 Cheyenne III. **DJM**

Piper PA-42 Cheyenne IIIA/400

Seven/ten-passenger corporate and commuter airline transport
and advanced trainer

Data for: Cheyenne IIIA

Powerplant: Two 537kW (720shp)
Pratt & Whitney PT6A-61 turboprops

Span: 14.53m (47ft 8in) (over tip tanks)

Length: 13.23m (43ft 4.75in)

Max cruise speed: 565km/h (351mph)

Accommodation: Seven/ten passengers plus one crew

First aircraft flown: 18 May 1979 (Cheyenne IIIA); 20 August 1969 (Cheyenne I)

History: The Cheyenne III is an 11-seat pressurised low-wing cabin turboprop based on a stretched Chieftain fuselage with PA-31T wings and large T-tail. Production: Cheyenne III/IIIA — 145; Cheyenne 400LS — 33. The Cheyenne III was developed from the I and II-XL, including increased wing span, lengthened fuselage, T-tail and more powerful engines. After the 89th Cheyenne III, production switched to the IIIA in 1983. Customs High Endurance Tracker (CHET) — aircraft fitted with special sensors delivered to the US Drug Enforcement Administration — used for a variety of day and night surveillance and identification missions. Cheyenne IV — later known as Cheyenne 400LS, first flew 23 February 1983. Similar to III but flush riveted throughout, wings adapted for 1,226.5kW (1,645shp) Garrett TPE331-14 engines, fuselage lengthened for increased pressurisation. Currently there are 189 Cheyenne Is; 17 IAs; 320 IIs; 79 IIXLs; 82 IIIs; 53 IIIAs and 29 400LSs registered as corporate aircraft.

Recognition: Low wing, with 45° sweep between fuselage and engine nacelles on leading edge — straight leading edge outboard of engines. Wing tip tanks. Long engine nacelles, mainly above wing and extending behind trailing edge. Long pointed nose. Slim fuselage. Swept tail fin with dorsal fillet and T-tail. Small ventral strake at rear. Four windows on port side of fuselage and five on starboard side. Passenger door at rear on port side.

Above:
Piper PA-44-180 Seminole. **PRM**

Below:
Piper PA-44-180 Seminole. **PRM**

Piper PA-44 Seminole

Twin-engined lightweight four-seat transport and corporate aircraft

Data for: Piper PA-44-180 Seminole
Powerplant: One each 134kW (180hp) Lycoming O-360-E1A6D and one LO-360-E1A6D contra-rotating piston engines
Span: 11.77m (38ft 7in)
Length: 8.41m (27ft 7in)
Max cruise speed: 309km/h (192mph)
Accommodation: Pilot plus three passengers
First aircraft flown: May 1976

History: Piper designed this new light twin in the mid-1970s to take the place of the Twin Comanche in its range of products. It featured the T-tail that was increasingly favoured by the American general aviation manufacturers and has a number of components fabricated from composites. Bearing a close resemblance to the Beech Duchess 76, the T-tail Seminole was one of a new generation of American twins intended for light transport duties, developed from the PA-28 Arrow. PA-44-180 Seminole — standard model; PA-44-180T Seminole — with 134.2kW (180hp) TO-360-E1AD/LTO-360-E1A6D turbocharged engines; Seminole production resumed in 1988. Over 480 built, with production continuing, and a small number are used as corporate aircraft.

Recognition: Twin-engined low-wing monoplane with T-tail. Retractable tricycle undercarriage. Slightly swept leading edge to wings with blunt tips. Three windows each side. Swept fin and rudder. Engine nacelles protrude slightly beyond wing trailing edge.

Above:
Piper PA-46-310P Malibu. **PRM**

Below:
Piper PA-46-310P Malibu. **PRM**

Piper PA-46 Malibu Mirage
Single-engined light pressurised-cabin business and corporate
aircraft

Data for: PA-46-350P Malibu Mirage
Powerplant: One 261kW (350hp) Textron Lycoming TIO-
540-AE2A turbocharged and intercooled flat-six piston engine
Span: 13.11m (43ft 0in)
Length: 8.72m (28ft 7.25in)
Max cruise speed: 430km/h (266mph)
Accommodation: Pilot plus five passengers
First aircraft flown: 30 November 1979
History: Introduced by Piper as the world's first pressurised cabin aircraft powered by a single piston engine and able
to operate at 7,620m (25,000ft). Original version PA-46-310 Malibu had a 231.3kW (310hp) Continental TSIO-
520-BE turbocharged engine. The PA-46-350P Malibu Mirage was introduced with the higher powered engine.
Production of the PA-46-310 was 402 when replaced by the PA-46-350P in 1988. Production of PA-46-350P is
continuing and some 175 had been built by early 1996, with many registered as corporate aircraft.
Recognition: Low-wing monoplane, with wings of equal taper and square tips. Retractable undercarriage. Deep
fuselage with pointed rear. Swept fin and rudder with small dorsal fillet. Tailplane set at fuselage extremity. Large
glazed cockpit area. Three oblong cabin windows each side, with port entry door level with wing trailing edge.
Unpressurised baggage compartment in nose.

Above:
Raytheon/Beechcraft Model 1900D. *via Mike Stroud*

Below:
Raytheon/Beechcraft Model 1900D. *Peter J. Cooper*

Raytheon/Beechcraft Model 1900D Execliner

Twin-turboprop regional and corporate transport
Data for: Model 1900D
Powerplant: Two 955kW (1,280 shp) Pratt & Whitney
Canada PT6A-67D turboprops
Span: 17.67m (57ft 11.8in) (over winglets)
Length: 17.63m (57ft 10in)
Max cruise speed: 511km/h (318mph)
Accommodation: 19 plus one/two crew
First aircraft flown: 1 March 1990

History: Developed from the Beechcraft Model 1900C Airliner and 1900 Executive-Liner — of which 255 were delivered between 1984 and 1991. The 1900C is a 1900 with starboard rear cargo door in place of an airstair. The C-1 has 'wet' wings with increased fuel and redesigned fuel system. The 1900D has a 14in deeper fuselage, new pressurisation, larger entry door, larger windows and wing tip winglets. Production: 1900 — 3; 1900C — 74; 1900C-1 — 180; 1900D — 125+. The 1900 was a 21-seat third level airliner/business aircraft based on the Model 200 with fuselage stretch, higher-powered engines, extra horizontal tail surfaces and tailplane finlets. Currently 15 1900 series are registered as corporate aircraft.

Recognition: Cranked leading edge of low-mounted high aspect ratio wing. Long, slim, oval fuselage with 'stand-up' cabin. Swept tailplane and fin. Each tailplane carries small ventral fin (taillet) near tip. Auxiliary horizontal fixed tail surface (stabilon) each side of rear fuselage. Twin ventral strakes. Small horizontal vortex generator on fuselage ahead of the wing roots. Eight small oval windows on each side.

Above:
Raytheon/Beechcraft 400A Beechjet. **Norman Pealing**

Below:
Raytheon/Beechcraft 400A Beechjet. **PRM**

Raytheon/Beechcraft 400A Beechjet

Twin-turbofan pressurised business and corporate aircraft

Data for: Beechjet 400A
Powerplant: Two 12.9kN (2,900lb st) Pratt & Whitney
Canada JT15D-5 turbofans   *Span:* 13.25m (43ft 6in)
Length: 14.75m (48ft 5in)
Max cruise speed: 834km/h (518mph)
Accommodation: Seven passengers plus two crew
First aircraft flown: 22 September 1989 (400A); 5 July 1991 (400T)

History: Beech reopened its interest in having a business jet in 1985 when it acquired all rights to the Mitsubishi Diamond light jet and put it into production with minor modifications as the Beechjet 400. Beechjet 400 was the initial production version based on the Mitsubishi Diamond II, acquired as shells from Mitsubishi and delivered from June 1986 until replaced by the 400A in November 1990. Beechjet 400T/T-1A Jayhawk is a Tanker Transport Training System (TTTS) aircraft for the USAF — 114 have been delivered. Currently 62 Beechjet 400s and 107 400As are registered to corporate users. Beech obtained 63 Mitsubishi MU-300 Diamond Is in component form which were fitted with modified internal trim and systems. 65 Model 400s were built and over 100 400As produced by late 1995; Diamond Is — 63; Diamond IAs — 27 and Diamond 2s — 8.

Recognition: Swept wing set low midway on fuselage. Small horizontal strakes on fuselage at base of fin. Small ventral fin. Twin engines mounted on sides of rear fuselage. Swept tail fin with swept T-tail. Small dorsal fairing on front base of fin. Round fuselage with small pointed nose. Six oval passenger windows on each side of fuselage. Forward entry door on port side.

Above:
Raytheon/Beechcraft 2000 Starship 1.
via *PRM*

Below:
Raytheon/Beechcraft 2000 Starship 1. *PRM*

Raytheon/Beechcraft 2000 Starship 1

Twin-turboprop business and corporate aircraft
Data for: 2000 Starship 1
Powerplant: Two 895kW (1,200shp)
Pratt & Whitney Canada PT6A-67A turboprops
Span: 16.60m (54ft 4.75in)
Length: 14.05m (46ft 1in)
Max cruise speed: 621km/h (386mph)
Accommodation: Seven plus one/two crew
First aircraft flown: 15 February 1986
History: Introduced as a 10-seat business
aircraft of all-composite construction and canard
design with two turboprops mounted on wing
in pusher configuration. 2000 Starship 1 —

43 built; 2000A — 7 built. Model 2000 — initial production version; Model 2000A — improved eight-seat version with new interior, extended range, increased take-off weight and stronger undercarriage. Currently all are registered as corporate aircraft, mainly in North America.

Recognition: Pusher turboprops with propellers aft of wing. Integral fuel tanks are separate structures forming root extensions bolted to main wing. Cylindrical cabin section mounted far forward of engines. Composite movable foreplane ahead of cockpit. No tailplane but 8ft winglets. Fuselage tapers to a point. Five large cabin windows on each side.

Above:
Raytheon/Beechcraft C90. **PRM**

Below:
Raytheon/Beechcraft 65-C90A King Air.
PRM

Raytheon/Beechcraft King Air C90B/King Air B90SE

Twin-turboprop pressurised business and corporate twin aircraft

Data for: King Air C90B
Powerplant: Two 410.0kW (550shp) Pratt & Whitney Canada PT6A-21 turboprops
Span: 15.32m (50ft 3in)
Length: 10.82m (35ft 6in)
Max cruise speed: 448km/h (278mph)
Accommodation: Up to 10 passengers plus 2 crew

First aircraft flown: King Air prototype — 20 January 1964; C90B — 1991

History: More than 1,300 Model 90 King Airs have been produced for commercial use. C90 — 496 built; C90-1 — 47; C90A — 228; C90B production continuing. 80 were in designated corporate use at the end of 1995, 48 in North America and 11 in Europe. Raytheon Aircraft introduced a reduced price King Air in July 1994, in a bid to stimulate demand for the aircraft. The B90SE (Special Edition) is essentially a reduced-specification C90B, lacking the current King Air's reduced-noise four-blade propellers and sound-absorbent cabin.

Recognition: Low-wing turboprop. Straight leading edge to wing, with fillet outboard of engines. Noticeable wing anhedral. Oval fuselage with short nose. Raised cockpit in line with engines. Swept tail fin, with pronounced dorsal fillet at base of leading edge. Swept tailplane set low on rear fuselage. Ventral strake under rear of pointed fuselage extremity. Three large oval windows plus small oval, aft of door (C90B).

Above:
Raytheon/Beechcraft B200 Super King Air. **PRM**

Below:
Raytheon/Beechcraft B200 Super King Air. **PRM**

Raytheon/Beechcraft Super King Air B200/B200SE

Twin-turboprop pressurised passenger, cargo or business light aircraft

Data for: Super King Air B200
Powerplant: Two 634kW (850shp) Pratt & Whitney Canada PT6A-42 turboprops
Span: 16.61m (54ft 6in)
Length: 13.34m (43ft 9in)
Max cruise speed: 536km/h (333mph)
Accommodation: 13 plus two crew   *First aircraft flown:* 27 October 1972 (Super King Air 200)
History: A stretched development of the King Air 90 and Model 100, the Model 200 was given a T-tail, more powerful engines and improved accommodation, to become the Model 200 Super King Air. Production: Model 200 — 833; 200C — 83; 200T — 38; 200CT — 4; A200 — 105; A200C — 66; A200CT — 43; B200 — 629 (continuing); B200C — 126; B200CT — 3; B200T — 13. 585 were flying in corporate aviation in late 1995; of these 359 were in North America, 83 in Europe and 51 in Africa. Super King Air B200C is a B200 with a 1.32m x 1.32m (4ft 4in x 4ft 4in) cargo door. Super King Air B200T has provision for removable tip tanks. B200CT combines tip tanks and cargo door as standard. 300LW is a lightweight version.
Recognition: Low-wing turboprop, with nacelles well ahead of leading edge of wing. Straight leading edge to wing, with fillet outboard of engines. Some versions feature wing tip tanks. Oval fuselage with short nose. Raised cockpit in line with engines. Swept tail fin, with pronounced dorsal fillet at base of leading edge. T-tailplane with small bullet fairing at top. Ventral strake under rear of pointed fuselage extremity. Six round and oval windows on each side. Door at rear of cabin on port side.

Above:
Raytheon/Beechcraft Super King Air 350. **PRM**

Right:
Raytheon/Beechcraft Super King Air 350. **PRM**

Raytheon/Beechcraft Super King Air 300LW/350

Twin-turboprop pressurised passenger cargo or business aircraft

Data for: Super King Air 350
Powerplant: Two 783kW (1,050shp) Pratt & Whitney Canada PT6A-60A turboprops
Span: 17.65m (57ft 11in) (over winglets)   *Length:* 14.22m (46ft 8in)
Max cruise speed: 547km/h (340mph)
Accommodation: Eight/12 plus two crew
First aircraft flown: September 1988
History: The Super King Air 300LW was a stretched and more powerful version of the original 300 introduced in 1988 for the European market. The 350 replaced the 300 in 1989 and was first delivered in March 1990. The 350C has a freight door and built-in airstair passenger door. Compared with the 300 and 350, has fuselage stretched 0.86m (2ft 10in) with NASA winglets and two additional cabin windows each side. In executive configuration it has double seating for eight passengers. 18 300s, 130 350s and nine 350Cs were registered to corporate users early in 1996.
Recognition: Low-wing turboprop, with nacelles well ahead of leading edge of wing. Straight leading edge to wing, with fillet outboard of engines. Small vertical winglets. Oval fuselage with short nose. Raised cockpit in line with engines. Swept tail fin, with pronounced dorsal fillet at base of leading edge. T-tailplane with small bullet fairing at top. Ventral strake under rear of pointed fuselage extremity. Eight oval windows on each side. Door at rear of cabin on port side.

Above:
Raytheon/Hawker 800. *via Mike Stroud*

Right:
Raytheon/Hawker 1000. *via PRM*

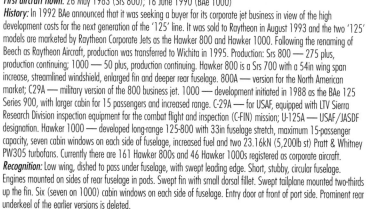

Raytheon/Hawker 800 and 1000
Twin-turbofan business transport and corporate aircraft
Data for: Hawker 800
Powerplant: Two 19.13kN (4,300lb st)
Garrett TFE731-5R-1H turbofans
Span: 15.66m (51ft 4.5in)   *Length:* 15.60m (51ft 2in)
Max cruise speed: 845km/h (525mph)   *Accommodation:* Two crew plus eight executive or 14 max
First aircraft flown: 26 May 1983 (Srs 800); 16 June 1990 (BAe 1000)
History: In 1992 BAe announced that it was seeking a buyer for its corporate jet business in view of the high
development costs for the next generation of the '125' line. It was sold to Raytheon in August 1993 and the two '125'
models are marketed by Raytheon Corporate Jets as the Hawker 800 and Hawker 1000. Following the renaming of
Beech as Raytheon Aircraft, production was transferred to Wichita in 1995. Production: Srs 800 — 275 plus,
production continuing; 1000 — 50 plus, production continuing. Hawker 800 is a Srs 700 with a 54in wing span
increase, streamlined windshield, enlarged fin and deeper rear fuselage. 800A — version for the North American
market; C29A — military version of the 800 business jet. 1000 — development initiated in 1988 as the BAe 125
Series 900, with larger cabin for 15 passengers and increased range. C-29A — for USAF, equipped with LTV Sierra
Research Division inspection equipment for the combat flight and inspection (C-FIN) mission; U-125A — USAF/JASDF
designation. Hawker 1000 — developed long-range 125-800 with 33in fuselage stretch, maximum 15-passenger
capacity, seven cabin windows on each side of fuselage, increased fuel and two 23.16kN (5,200lb st) Pratt & Whitney
PW305 turbofans. Currently there are 161 Hawker 800s and 46 Hawker 1000s registered as corporate aircraft.
Recognition: Low wing, dished to pass under fuselage, with swept leading edge. Short, stubby, circular fuselage.
Engines mounted on sides of rear fuselage in pods. Swept fin with small dorsal fillet. Swept tailplane mounted two-thirds
up the fin. Six (seven on 1000) cabin windows on each side of fuselage. Entry door at front of port side. Prominent rear
underkeel of the earlier versions is deleted.

Above:
Reims Cessna F406 Caravan II. **PRM**

Below:
Reims Cessna F406 Caravan II. **DJM**

Reims Cessna F406 Caravan II

Twin-turboprop unpressurised light business, utility transport and corporate aircraft
Data for: F406 Caravan II
Powerplant: Two 373kW (500shp) Pratt & Whitney Canada PT6A-112 turboprops
Span: 15.08m (49ft 5.5in)
Length: 11.89m (39ft 0.25in)
Max cruise speed: 424km/h (263mph)
Accommodation: Nine passengers plus two crew; six in VIP version

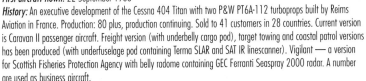

First aircraft flown: 22 September 1983
History: An executive development of the Cessna 404 Titan with two P&W PT6A-112 turboprops built by Reims Aviation in France. Production: 80 plus, production continuing. Sold to 41 customers in 28 countries. Current version is Caravan II passenger aircraft. Freight version (with underbelly cargo pod), target towing and coastal patrol versions has been produced (with underfuselage pod containing Terma SLAR and SAT IR linescanner). Vigilant — a version for Scottish Fisheries Protection Agency with belly radome containing GEC Ferranti Seaspray 2000 radar. A number are used as business aircraft.
Recognition: Developed from the Cessna Conquest airframe. Low-wing twin-engined monoplane. Single swept fin and rudder with dorsal fillet forward of fin. Square wing tips. Straight leading edge to wing. Engine nacelles over wing protrude behind trailing edge. Twin ventral strakes at rear. Dihedralled tailplane set midway up fin. Four oblong cabin windows, together with two smaller windows, on each side of fuselage.

Above:
Rockwell Turbo Commander 690. **PRM**

Below:
Rockwell/Gulfstream Commander 695A. **PRM**

Rockwell 690A Turbo Commander

Six/seven-seat corporate and business aircraft
Data for: 690A Turbo Commander
Powerplant: Two 522kW (700shp)
Garrett AiResearch TPE331-5-251K turboprops
Span: 14.22m (46ft 8in)
Length: 13.52m (44ft 4.25in)
Max cruise speed: 465km/h (289mph)
Accommodation: Six/seven including pilot
First aircraft flown: 31 December 1964 (680V);
3 March 1969 (680T); June 1972 (690A)
History: A turboprop version of the original Aero
Commander L-3805 design by Ted Smith. Aero

Commander became part of North American (subsequently Rockwell International and Gulfstream). Larger and more powerful versions of the basic Aero Commander high-wing twin-engined design appeared as the Model 680, 685, 690, 695 and 720. Other versions are the 900, 980, 1000 and 1200. The high wing layout is relatively unusual among business twins but in early 1996 there were 466 Turbo Commanders registered to corporate users.
Recognition: Twin-engined high-wing monoplane. Straight leading edge to high aspect ratio wings. Slim turboprop engines but with square nacelle protruding behind trailing edge of wing. Slightly swept tail fin with small dorsal fillet. Diamond shaped tailplane, with anhedral, mounted at extremity of rear tapered fuselage. Prominent glazed cockpit area with side cabin windows of varying sizes.

Above:
Saab SF340A. **PRM**

Below:
Saab SF340A. **Peter J. Cooper**

Saab 340

Twin-turboprop regional airliner and corporate transport
Data for: Saab SF340B
Powerplant: Two 1,393kW (1,870shp)
General Electric CT7-9B turboprops
Span: 21.44m (70ft 4in)
Length: 19.73m (64ft 8.75in)
Max cruise speed: 522km/h (325mph)
Accommodation: 30/37 plus two crew
First aircraft flown: 25 January 1983 (340);
April 1989 (340B)

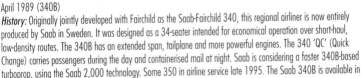

History: Originally jointly developed with Fairchild as the Saab-Fairchild 340, this regional airliner is now entirely produced by Saab in Sweden. It was designed as a 34-seater intended for economical operation over short-haul, low-density routes. The 340B has an extended span, tailplane and more powerful engines. The 340 'QC' (Quick Change) carries passengers during the day and containerised mail at night. Saab is considering a faster 340B-based turboprop, using the Saab 2,000 technology. Some 350 in airline service late 1995. The Saab 340B is available in corporate form. Four Saab 340As are operating in corporate aviation.
Recognition: Slim engines projecting forward of low, straight wing which is set midway along circular-section fuselage. Swept fin and rudder with dorsal fillet projecting forward to the cabin windows. Small, dihedralled tailplane is mounted either side of tail cone below fin. Cockpit windscreen slopes down to nose cone in continuous line.

Above:
Socata TBM 700. **PRM**

Below:
Socata TBM 700. **PRM**

Socata TBM 700

Single-turboprop pressurised business
and corporate aircraft
Data for: TBM 700
Powerplant: One 522kW (700shp)
Pratt & Whitney Canada PT6A-64
turboprop
Span: 12.16m (39ft 10.75in)
Length: 10.43m (34ft 2.5in)
Max cruise speed: 555km/h (345mph)
Accommodation: Four/five passengers
plus one/two crew

First aircraft flown: 14 July 1988
History: Aérospatiale General Aviation Division was inspired by the Mooney M.301 project and started as a co-operative venture between Aérospatiale and Mooney for an eight-seat pressurised single-engined business turboprop. Mooney subsequently pulled out in 1991. Approximately 110 had been built by the end of 1995 and 75 are registered as business aircraft.
Recognition: Straight leading edge, with square tips, to low-mounted wing. Noticeable dihedral. Sweptback fin — with dorsal fillet. Non-swept tailplane set at rear fuselage extremity. Twin strakes under rear fuselage. Four cabin windows on each side of fuselage. Entry door to rear of wing trailing edge, on port side. Bullet fairing on port wing leading edge, near to tip. Long nose to accommodate turboprop, with prominent exhausts each side.

Above:
WSK PZL-Mielec M-20 Mewa. **PRM**

WSK PZL-Mielec M-20 Mewa

Twin-engined executive transport, liaison, survey and ambulance aircraft
Data for: M-20 Mewa (Gull)
Powerplant: Two 164kW (220hp) Teledyne Continental
TSIO/LTSIO-360-KB turbocharged piston engines
Span: 11.86m (38ft 11in)
Length: 8.72m (28ft 7.25in)
Max cruise speed: 360km/h (223mph)
Accommodation: Four/five passengers plus one crew
First aircraft flown: 25 July 1979 (Polish prototype)
History: PZL sought to acquire production licences for Western aircraft and in 1976 negotiated with Piper Aircraft
to produce the PA-34 Seneca II from Piper-provided kits — powered by two PZL-built Franklin 6A-350-C engines.
Exported as the M-20 Gemini. A batch of 15 M-20-03s was built for customers in Austria, Germany, India and
Turkey. 15 were delivered to South Africa. 20 are in use by Polish First Aid Aviation Service. M-20-00 and M-20-01
were original versions in the 1980s. M-20-03 is the current version. M-20-04 has strengthened wing and increased
take-off weight. South African aircraft known as TM20B Flamingo II were originally built to accept Polish-built PZL-F
engines. A small number are registered as corporate aircraft.
Recognition: Twin-engined low-wing monoplane. Engines set high on leading edge of wings. Long pointed nose.
Tapering fuselage. Four cabin windows on each side. Wings of parallel chord with rounded tips. Pronounced fillet
at front wing root. Swept fin and rudder. Low-mounted oblong tailplane.

Above:
Agusta A109A II. **PRM**

Below:
Agusta A109A. **PRM**

Agusta A109C

Twin-engined light general purpose and
corporate helicopter
Data for: Agusta A109C
Powerplant: Two 335kW (450shp) Allison
250-C20R turboshafts
Main rotor diameter: 22.0m (36ft 1in)
Length: 13.05m (42ft 9.75in)
(rotors turning)
Max cruise speed: 285km/h (177mph)
Accommodation: Crew of one or two plus
six passengers

First aircraft flown: 4 August 1971 (A109A); April 1983 (A109K)

History: Agusta of Italy acquired a licence to build Bell helicopters in 1952. Some versions of Sikorsky are built under
licence. The A109 multi-role helicopter is its own design and manufacture. A109A — original production version;
A109A Mk II — introduced 1981; A109C — executive version; A109K2 — for 'hot and high' operations with two
575kW (771shp) Turboméca Arriel K1 turboshafts. Also produced as a special civil rescue version. Many are in use as
corporate helicopters.

Recognition: Short nose with upswept cabin. Enclosed turboshafts on cabin roof with fairing for main rotor shaft. Four-
bladed main rotor. Fully retractable undercarriage. Flat fuselage floor to cabin with upward taper to rear fuselage.
Large thin swept dorsal fin and small swept ventral fin. Two-blade rear rotor set on port side of rear fuselage extremity.

Above:
Bell 206B JetRanger II. ***PRM***

Below:
Bell 206 JetRanger III. ***PRM***

Bell 206 JetRanger

General purpose light commercial and corporate helicopter

Data for: Bell Model 206B JetRanger III

Powerplant: One 313kW (420shp)
Allison 250-C20J turboshaft

Main rotor diameter: 10.16m (33ft 4in)

Length: 11.82m (38ft 9.5in) (rotors turning)

Max cruise speed: 216km/h (134mph)

Accommodation: Pilot plus up to four passengers

First aircraft flown: 10 January 1966 (JetRanger I); 1976 (JetRanger III)

History: The original Model 206A remained in production until 1972, when 660 had been built. The 206B JetRanger II entered production in 1971 and a total of 1,619 were delivered. Production was transferred to Mirabel in Canada in 1986 and production continues of approximately seven per month. Nearly 7,500 JetRangers had been produced by Bell and licences by early 1996, including some 2,000 military OH-58 series. 206A — original production version with 236kW (317shp) Allison 250-C18A; 206B JetRanger II — with 298.2kW (400shp) Allison 250-C20; 206B JetRanger III — with 313.2kW (420shp) Allison 250-C20J; OH-58 Kiowa — military variant of the JetRanger with 313.2kW (420shp) Allison T63-A-720; Bell 407 is a new light-turbine helicopter. The single-engined 407 and twin-turbine 407T are based on the current model 206, with the four-blade rotor dynamic system from the OH-58D Kiowa Warrior. The JetRanger has also been made under licence by Agusta in Italy with some 1,000 built, and production continuing. It has become one of the most widely used helicopters on the civil market.

Recognition: Enclosed turboshaft above cabin. Large glazed cabin windows and pointed nose. Tail boom has small tailplane half-way along empennage and swept dorsal/ventral fin. Twin-blade main rotor. Skid undercarriage.

Above:
Bell 206L-3 LongRanger III. **PRM**

Below:
Bell 206L-3 LongRanger III. **PRM**

Bell 206L-3 LongRanger

Stretched turbine-powered general purpose light and corporate helicopter
Data for: LongRanger III
Powerplant: One 485kW (650shp) Allison 250-C30P turboshaft
Main rotor diameter: 11.28m (37ft 0in)
Length: 13.02m (42ft 8.5in) (rotors turning)
Max cruise speed: 203km/h (126mph)
Accommodation: Five passengers plus two crew

First aircraft flown: 11 September 1974 (LongRanger I)

History: Designed to satisfy a requirement for a turbine-powered general purpose helicopter in a size and performance range between the five-seat JetRanger II and 15-seat Model 205A-1. Developed from the JetRanger II with an 0.64m (2ft 1in) longer fuselage. Production moved to Canada in January 1987. The Model 406 Combat Scout is a simplified combat helicopter. Current production version, in Canada, is the Model 206L-3 LongRanger III. A large number are registered as corporate helicopters.

Recognition: Has longer fuselage than JetRanger with additional pair of cabin windows. Bell Noda-Matic transmission. Endplate fins on tailplane. Double doors on port side. Tubular skid-type landing gear. Swept dorsal and ventral tail fin. Two-blade main rotor. Two-blade tail rotor on port side of rear fuselage.

Above:
Bell 412. *via Mike Stroud*

Below:
Bell 412. *via Mike Stroud*

Bell 212 Twin Two-Twelve/412HP

Twin-turbine utility and corporate helicopter
Data for: Twin Two-Twelve
Powerplant: Pratt & Whitney Canada PT6T-3B Turbo Twin-PAC, 961.9kW (1,290shp) comprising two PT6 turboshafts coupled to combining gearbox with single output shaft
Main rotor diameter: 14.69m (48ft 2.25in) (with tracking tips)
Length: 17.46m (57ft 3.25in) (rotors turning)
Max cruise speed: 189km/h (117mph)
Accommodation: 14 passengers plus one crew
First aircraft flown: 1968
History: The Canadian Government gave approval in 1968 to develop a twin-engined UH-1 with P&WC PT6-3. Manufacture transferred to Canada in August 1988 and production is two per month. Twin Two-Twelve — civil version; CH-135 — Canadian version, originally CUH-1N; UH-1N — US Air Force, Navy and Marines version. Model 412HP — is the four-blade version and improved transmission; Model 412SP — Special Performance version, in production in Indonesia, with different seating option and greater fuel capacity; Agusta Griffon — Italian Agusta-developed military version, N Bell — 412 — licence-built by IPTN in Indonesia. The Agusta-Bell 212 is produced in Italy by Agusta — the 212ASW being for the Italian Navy, Turkey and Iran. A number are in use as corporate helicopters.
Recognition: Two-bladed, semi-rigid teetering main rotor (four-blade on 412). Tubular skid-type landing gear. Lock-on ground wheels. Can be fitted with floats. Large passenger cabin, with sliding doors. Long rear fuselage terminating in small fin with two-blade tail rotor on starboard side of fin. Small fixed tailplane, with square tips, three-quarters along fuselage rear.

Above:
Bell 222. **PRM**

Below:
Bell 222. **PRM**

Bell 222

Twin-turbine light commercial and corporate helicopter
Data for: Bell 222
Powerplant: Two 489.9kW (657shp) Avco Lycoming LTS 101-650C-2 turboshafts
Main rotor diameter: 12.12m (39ft 9in)
Length: 12.50m (41ft 0in)
Max cruise speed: 265km/h (165mph)
Accommodation: Seven/nine passengers plus one crew
First aircraft flown: 13 August 1976
History: In April 1974, Bell decided to build the Model 222 as the first light twin-engined helicopter to be built in the USA. Production ceased in 1989 after 184 had been built. The type was produced in three versions — the basic Model 222B, the 222B Executive and the 222UT (with skid undercarriage). Offshore versions have emergency flotation gear, auxiliary fuel tanks and are equipped for two-pilot IFR operations over the sea. The Executive incorporated many refinements. The majority of the 222s on the civil register are used as corporate helicopters.

Recognition: Elegant lines of fuselage and retractable undercarriage. Bell's focused pylon and Noda-Matic cabin suspension system. Stub wings (sponsons) carry main wheels. Two-blade main rotor. Downward viewing windows of flight deck for rooftop landings. Tailplane mounted midway along the rear fuselage and fitted with endplate fins. Dorsal and ventral fins. Tail rotor fitted on port fuselage extremity.

Above:
Aérospatiale AS355F1 Twin Squirrel. **PRM**

Below:
Aérospatiale AS350B Ecureuil. **PRM**

Eurocopter (Aérospatiale) AS350 Ecureuil/AS355 Ecureuil 2

Single/Twin-turboshaft light general purpose and corporate helicopter

Data for: Aérospatiale AS350BA Ecureuil (Squirrel)
Powerplant: One 478kW (641shp) Turboméca Arriel 1B turboshaft
Main rotor diameter: 10.69m (35ft 1in)
Length: 12.94m (42ft 5.5in) (rotors turning)
Max cruise speed: 234km/h (145mph)
Accommodation: Pilot plus four/five passengers
First aircraft flown: 27 June 1974 (AS350);
28 September 1979 (AS355)
History: The Ecureuil (Squirrel) was designed as a
replacement for the Alouette III. AS350B — original

production version; AS350BA — current version; AS350B2 — powered by 546kW (732shp) Arriel 1D1. Known as Super Star in North America; AS350D AStar — exclusively for US market with Textron Lycoming LTS 101-600A-3 turboshaft engine; AS355E Twinstar — for US market with two 316.9kW (425shp) 250-C20F turboshaft engines; AS355F Ecureuil 2 (Twin Squirrel) — European version with two 343kW (460shp) Allison 250-C20R turboshaft engines; AS355N Ecureuil 2 — current civil production version with two 340kW (456shp) Turboméca TM319 IM Arrius turboshafts; AS550 Fennec — military version of AS350B2. A very popular helicopter for UK corporate users.

Recognition: Streamlined cabin with glazed upper half. Enclosed engine/engines on roof of cabin. Short main shaft holding three-bladed main rotor. Skid undercarriage. Long slender fuselage with small swept dorsal and ventral fin. Small oblong tailplane set three-quarters along rear fuselage. Two-bladed rear rotor, set on starboard side.

Above:
Aerospatiale SA365N Dauphin 2. **DJM**

Below:
Aérospatiale SA365N Dauphin 2. **PRM**

Eurocopter (Aérospatiale) AS365N Dauphin 2

Twin-turbine commercial general purpose and corporate helicopter
Data for: AS365N2 Dauphin 2
Powerplant: Two 551kW (739shp) Turboméca Arriel 1C2 turboshafts
Main rotor diameter: 11.94m (39ft 2in)
Length: 13.68m (44ft 10.55in) (rotors turning)
Max cruise speed: 285km/h (177mph)
Accommodation: VIP version four/six passengers plus one crew
First aircraft flown: 2 June 1972 (SA360); 28 January 1975 (SA365)
History: The original Dauphin 1 was designed by Aérospatiale as a replacement for the widely used Alouette. AS365N2 Dauphin 2 is the current production model. AS366G1 (HH-65A Dolphin) — 101 supplied to the US Coast Guard. AS565UA/AA/CA Panther — French Army version; AS565MA/SA Panther — naval versions; Ambulance/EMS — with stretchers; Offshore Support — 13 passengers, autopilot and navigation systems, pop-out floats. Produced in China as Harbin Z-9. The original Dauphin 1 was powered by a single 782.9kW (1,050shp) Astazou XVIIIA turboshaft. Has been delivered to 44 countries and a large number are used as business helicopters.
Recognition: Confusing because it is also called Dauphin 2, the 365N is a major redesign compared with the SA365C. Side-by-side engines, with stainless steel firewall between them, mounted above canopy. Eleven-blade Fenestron at rear. Four-blade main rotors. Tail fin above Fenestron. Tailplane with fins at extremity. Retractable undercarriage.

Above:
Westland SA341G Gazelle I. **PRM**

Below:
Aérospatiale SA341G Gazelle I. Oliver March

Eurocopter (Aérospatiale/Westland) SA341/342 Gazelle

Single-engined utility and business helicopter
Data for: Eurocopter SA342 Gazelle
Powerplant: One 640kW (858shp) Turboméca Astazou XIV turboshaft
Main rotor diameter: 10.50m (34ft 5.5in)
Length: 11.97m (39ft 5.3in) (rotors turning)
Max cruise speed: 260km/h (161mph)
Accommodation: Pilot plus up to four passengers
First aircraft flown: 7 April 1967

History: The initial design was for a utility/general purpose helicopter for the French (built by Aérospatiale) and British armed services (built by Westland). Exported to armed forces in a number of countries, it is now also in commercial use around the world. SA341B, C, D and E versions for British armed forces; SA341F for French Army; SA341G and SA342J — civilian versions; SA342K, L and M — military versions; SA342M Viviane — for night military operations. It remains in low rate production and 19 are civil registered in the UK. 628 SA341s were built and over 640 SA342s delivered by early 1996.

Recognition: Streamlined glazed cabin with exposed turboshaft on roof behind rotor shaft. Three-bladed main rotor on short main shaft. Undercarriage skids. Upward sloping rear fuselage with enclosed tail rotor at base of swept fin. Small oblong tailplane with square tips. Pronounced exhaust pipe at rear of engine.

Above:
MBB BO 105.

Below:
Eurocopter BO 105. **PRM**

Eurocopter (MBB) BO 105

Light utility and corporate helicopter
Data for: BO 105CB
Powerplant: Two 313kW (420shp) Allison 250-C20
turboshafts
Main rotor diameter: 9.84m (32ft 3.5in)
Length: 11.86m (38ft 11in) (including main and tail rotor)
Max cruise speed: 242km/h (150mph)
Accommodation: Pilot plus four passengers *First aircraft flown:* 16 February 1967

History: A number of different versions have been built since it was introduced by MBB in 1967, but all are basically similar in external appearance. Main production source is Eurocopter Deutschland, but Spanish models assembled by CASA, Indonesian models manufactured and assembled by IPTN and BO 105LS exclusively manufactured by Eurocopter Canada. BO 105C — original standard production model; BO 105CB — production model from 1975; BO 105CBS — with 10in longer fuselage and increased seating capacity; BO 105D/DBS — UK market production versions; BO 105LS — 'hot and high' version with two 410kW (550shp) Allison 250-C28C turboshafts; BO 105/PAH-1/VBH/BSH-1 — military variants of BO 105 produced exclusively by Eurocopter Canada. More than 1,500 BO 105s of all models have been delivered to 39 countries and it is a popular corporate helicopter.

Recognition: Deep oval squat cabin with skid undercarriage. Rounded glazed nose. Four-blade main rotor. Rear fuselage extends from top rear of cabin and features small tailplane with oblong fins at extremities. Swept tailplane with two-blade tail rotor affixed at tip.

Above:
McDonnell Douglas MD500N NOTAR. **PRM**

Below:
Hughes 500D. **DJM**

Hughes 369/McDonnell Douglas 500/530

Light turbine-powered utility and corporate helicopter
Data for: McDonnell Douglas MD500E
Powerplant: One 313kW (420shp) Allison 250-C20B
or 335.6kW (450shp) 250-C20R turboshaft
Main rotor diameter: 8.05m (26ft 5in)
Length: 8.61m (28ft 3in) (rotors turning)
Max cruise speed: 248km/h (154mph)
Accommodation: Pilot and up to six passengers
First aircraft flown: 27 February 1963 (Hughes YOH-6A);
13 September 1966 (Hughes 369A); 23 February 1970

(500C); 28 January 1982 (500E); 22 October 1982 (530F)
History: Hughes Helicopters Inc became a subsidiary of McDonnell Douglas Corporation in January 1984 and the
name changed to McDonnell Douglas Helicopter Company in August 1985. Hughes OH-6A — production version for
US Army; Hughes 369A Model 500 — civil version of OH-6A; Model 500C — more powerful 400shp Allison 250-
C20 turbine; Model 500D — introduced five-blade main rotor and T-tail; 420hp Allison; Model 500E/MD500E —
pointed nose and larger tail endplates; MD520L — new rotors; MD530F Lifter — 650shp Allison 250-C30 and
bigger rotors; MD530N NOTAR — no tail rotor and twin vertical fins; MD900/901 Explorer — eight-seat, twin-
engined version with no tail rotor and twin vertical fins. Model 500/300 Defender — military derivative of
MD500/530. More than 4,600 Model 500/530 series produced by early 1996 and many in use as corporate
helicopters.
Recognition: Four-blade main rotor on 369/500 (five-blade on 520/530) above bubble cabin with pointed front
and rear ends. Tall double-braced landing skids. Narrowing, slim tail boom with four-blade rotor on port side. T-tail
with small end plates and ventral fin — optional four-blade Quiet Knight tail rotor.

Above:
Sikorsky S-76B. **PRM**

Below:
Sikorsky S-76A II Plus. **PRM**

Sikorsky S-76B
Twin-turbine offshore support, business transport and corporate helicopter
Data for: S-76B
Powerplant: Two 732kW (981shp) Pratt & Whitney Canada PT6B-36A turboshafts
Main rotor diameter: 13.41m (44ft 0in)
Length: 16.00m (52ft 6in) (rotors turning)
Max cruise speed: 269km/h (166mph)
Accommodation: Executive four/eight passengers plus two crew

First aircraft flown: 22 June 1984 (MkII); 1977 (Mk I)
History: Designed for offshore support, business transport, medical evacuation and general utility purposes using technology and aerodynamics based on those of the UH-60 Black Hawk. In addition to the USA it has been exported to China, Germany, Japan, Netherlands, South Korea and the UK. The S-76 Mk II remains in production. The S-76 Utility and S-76B have the PT6B engine. The S-76C, which first flew on 18 May 1990, is powered by two 539kW (723shp) Turboméca Arriel 1S1 turboshafts. H-76 is the armed utility model named Eagle and the H-76N a naval variant. A number are in use as corporate helicopters.
Recognition: Four-blade main rotor with high twist and varying section. Four-blade cross-beam tail rotor on port side. Twin engines above cabin. Long sleek fuselage. Retractable undercarriage. Four windows, of varying shapes, on each side of fuselage.

INDEX